GW01459100

Off The Beaten Track...
Canal Carping

By Rob Maylin and friends

Bountyhunter
Publications

First published in 2015
By Bountyhunter Publications

ISBN 978-0-9932228-2-5
Originated in Great Britain

Contents

Introduction by Rob Maylin 4

Chapter 1 Tactics and Techniques
Canal Technical by Danny Champion 7

Chapter 2 The Royal Military Canal
A Tale of Two Records by Bill Phillips 29
The Town Stretch by Ken South 87

Chapter 3 The Chelmer and Blackwater Canal
Mystery and Secrets by Matt Lee 98
Canal Life by Jade Martin 108
A Whole New World by Matt Lee 116

Chapter 4 Canal Catches 124

Chapter 5 Cheshire Canal
Canal Capers by Lee Colford 165

Chapter 6 The Dudley Canal
The Black Country Cut by Josh Myatt 174
The Dudley Canal System by Darren Dunn & Anthony Williamson 179
Urban Legends by Craig McEvoy 182

Chapter 7 The Sankey Canal
The Unstable Campaign by Lee Colford 198

Chapter 8 The South Holland Main Drain
South Holland Main Drain Carp by Liam Chapman 213

Chapter 9 The Wryley and Essington Canal
The Wryley and Essington Canal by Neil Horton 221

Chapter 10 The Grand Union Canal
Grand Carping by Dan Cleary 250
Grand Union Canal Cracker by Dan Sibley 260
Unknown Possibilities by Keith William 263
Colne Valley Escapees by Nick Helleur 268
Basingstoke Canal Record by Danny Champion 274

Chapter 11 Overseas Canal Carping
A Tale of Three Fifties by Dan Cleary 289

INTRODUCTION

By Rob Maylin

Canal carping has become one of the fastest growing areas of carp fishing in recent years in the UK, not that there's anything new in carp fishing canals, as this book will soon prove. Some carp anglers have been fishing canals almost exclusively for decades, and of course canal carping in countries like Holland and Belgium is commonplace. In fact many European anglers from England and further afield travel to these two counties in search of the huge specimens that inhabit them. This book focuses on English canal carp angling with just a couple of examples of what is available if you wish to travel.

Canal carping is, as you would expect, a little different to still water or river carping in that these vast waterways can stretch for miles, some stretches separated by locks that somehow even the carp manage to transverse. Therefore I thought it important to have a technical 'how to do it' chapter with all the latest techniques including underwater cameras and long-range baiting spoons. I chose Danny Champion, who appears later in this book with his Basingstoke record capture on that stretch of the Grand Union Canal. In this you will find location, watercraft, tackle, tactics and techniques in great detail and with superb photography.

We are very fortunate to have articles featuring no less than four canal records, topped by a fantastic life history by BCSG member Bill Phillips. Bill holds not one but two different canal records and has been fishing and writing about canal carping for over forty years. The catalyst for compiling this book was a photo Bill sent to me in 2014 of him with a 47lb fully scaled mirror, an incredible beast of a carp, perfectly proportioned, and a huge fish by canal standards. I contacted Bill only to find that he had in fact caught this fish on numerous occasions, originally at double figures and through its twenties, thirties and a few times at forty-plus... more importantly from stretches of the canal miles apart! Bill graciously offered to tell us his story, and it appears here in full, an amazing part of English carp fishing history. I cannot thank him enough.

Also within these covers are some words from prolific canal carper, Nick Helleur. Nick has also fished the canal for over thirty years and during that time has pursued not only the native specimens but some huge escapees from Savay and other Colne Valley venues. These captures are topped off by an incredible Savay linear in the upper thirties, the Uxbridge section of the Grand Union Canal record, a huge framed 42lb'er caught by Dan Smith.

It's hardly surprising that canal carping has become one of the fastest growing areas of carp fishing when you see the size of some of the carp swimming in our canal systems. Not only that, but since many of these canal fish are escapees from the many still waters that line the banks of our canals, the variety of strains is incredible. They include anything from brightly coloured Koi carp carelessly dropped into the canal when they got too big for the aquarium or garden pond they were in, to ghost carp, big leathery battle-scared warriors, long linear type Leneys from the Colne valley to huge fully scaled mirrors nearing fifty pounds. I have never seen a proper book devoted to canal carping, so as part of our 'Off The Beaten

Track' series, I decided it was about time I rectified this.

Also in this book long-term canal angler Dan Cleary relays his canal life story. Ken South tells the tale of his canal fishing, culminating in the capture of a huge Royal Military canal common. Canal carpers Matt Lee, Jade Martin, Nick Mays, Neil Horton, Josh Myatt, Keith Williams, James Willets, Liam Webster, Liam Chapman, Dan Sibley,, Luke Sparkes any may others all contribute their own personal accounts on our British canal systems including The Royal Military Canal, The Chelmer and Blackwater Canal, North West Canal, Grantham Lincolnshire Canal, Staffs Canal, The Trent and Mersey Canal, The Worcester Canal, The Walsall Canal, Nottingham Canal, Stainforth and Keadby, Cheshire Canal, The Dudley Canal, The South Holland Main Drain, The Wryley and Essington Canal and of course the Grand Union. A huge variety of canals with one common denominator... dedicated canal carpers!

Finally it did not seem right somehow to not include a small overseas chapter. The Dutch and Belgian carp anglers have concentrated their angling on the vast canal systems which crisscross these countries for decades, and some of the catches have been legendary, so much so that many English anglers have crossed the channel to chance their luck in search of these European beasts. There are too many to mention here, but Nick Helleur, Dan Cleary, Bill Phillips and even my old Savay companions Bruce Ashby and John Harry have made many visits. I chose Dan Cleary whose 'Tale of Three Fifties' in Belgium will no doubt encourage even more canal carpers to make the journey in search of monster canal specimens abroad.

Chapter 1

Tactics and Techniques

Canal Technical

By Danny Champion

Canal carping is almost ignored these days as the day tickets become a playground for the glory hunters try to catch the same fish. The meaning of a large specimen of true value is truly lost. I see canal carping as a way back into the old school days of carp fishing, the simple and unknown. Never in my life did I think I would catch a canal 40; it was one of those moments in my life I'd never forget. I never set out to catch it but the more time I spent looking for carp the more I got to know about her (Split Tail). She had a tail the width of a dustbin lid with pectoral fins a foot long, and her long, grey body was battered with scars from years of swimming along an old canal – a true warrior of the channel. This is the kind of fish that deserves the right to be called a specimen; she wasn't bred in a fish farm and fed on pellets all her life but had to search and eat naturals to survive in a place that not many can grow in. most of her brothers and sisters have been taken away and eaten by poachers. I was asked by Rob Maylin to write this article on the technical side of carp fishing, and I had to think long and hard about whether I wanted to write and share the information that I have collected over my search for the unknown, as not everyone has the same views as I have. Canals can be literally taken apart in months by anglers taking all kind of fish away to eat. And yes, this happens in this day and age. But I thought to myself the more anglers on the canal that are just as passionate about the fishing as I am will not only protect the fish stock but help the fish grow and be able to keep an accurate record of the stocks. I hope the information you read will help you unlock your local canal. Be aware it's not for the fainthearted but well worth the wait.

The first thing I will talk about is the best time to start your campaign and how to get the basic information you will need along with the best ways to remember the important information. January is probably the best time to start preparing for your season on the canal. I find January extremely hard fishing, so I tend to write this month off. Canals are extremely hard to get to grips with remembering locations, so it's well worth buying a diary to keep notes and photos in. I would start by looking on old forums to find out the basics.

Most canals have long history of diehard carp anglers who spend years searching for the unknown. These forums will give you a good idea on the fish stocks and locations. Although the information will be old, it will get you started. Sometimes you will find the odd photo amongst the forums. Print these out and stick them in your diary with the weights written on the back so you can start to put the puzzle of the canal together. Facebook is one of the most annoying sites on the Internet, yet is can be extremely helpful. Most canals have a Facebook group here you will find up-to-date catch reports. Now if you're like me I spend at least five hours a week in my local tackle shop, which is another good place to find out more information. Don't ignore the match anglers – their numbers are far greater than carp anglers, and they are not as secret squirrel as most carp anglers.

So now you have research the canal from what other people have had to say. I suggest looking on Google Maps. You will probably find it hard seeing the water from the maps, as the trees seem to cover everywhere bar the turning bays and flashes. Still, this is vital, as most of the fish will be in these turning bays. I wouldn't jump ahead and try to cover all the canal on your first year. When I first started I did a five-mile stretch closest to my house, which gave me more than enough water to cover. I would write in your diary the nearest roads to each turning bay and give each one a name or number. By doing this you will be able to keep an accurate record of fish sightings and catch reports. I would also look for where I could park, as some stretches can be anything up to two miles before the next road or track. I can tell you from my own fishing that the warmer months tend to produce more bites, as most of the canals are very shady. This means the water can take longer to warm up. In turn the carp in the Basingstoke canal spawn a lot later in the year. In 2015 the fish spawned in the second week of July, a week after I had Split Tail out at 40lb 2oz, and she was full of spawn. I know this for a fact, as the week after I fished the same spot and had a very worn out 35lb 6oz common. She obviously had just finished releasing her eggs and needed a good meal, but she was the only female I landed in that session. I had six other fish, but they were all immature males ranging from low doubles to mid twenties.

Once you have completed your research I would then start looking at locating the carp on the canal. What you will read in the next few pages is what I've found on my local canal. You might find it different on your local, but as a whole this information should put you on the right spots. Locating carp on canals has always puzzled me, but once you've been walking along the canal for a few miles you always see them, especially in the warmer months. A good place to start is to just go for a walk. I'd think nothing of walking the canal footpaths for the afternoon racking up over eight miles. For the older generation I suggest riding a bike. This is the quickest way, but I think you can miss a lot, and you can spook the fish! The far side of the canal is always where you will spot the carp under the overhanging trees. Failing this, I'd suggest looking around the turning bays. The fish will most likely be cruising the opposite bank. I believe they do this to get away from all the noise a vibrations on the footpath side, but be aware that turning bays can end up being a prime spot for fly tipping, so you may have a lot of work to do before you start, and as the name suggest narrow boats can be a nightmare in the summer months turning in these bays!

Now, the flashes on the canals can be amazing places in the winter if your canal is shallow. With a deep flash you can be sure most of the fish will be in this area. The Ash Vale flash near Aldershot is a prime example of this. I wouldn't suggest casting to the far side of the flash, as the carp will be used to the fact that people feed the ducks on the footpath, creating an ideal prebaited area for anglers, but the downside to this would be the fact the ducks know this, and you will more than likely end up hooking a duck or two. This can be a big problem, as in the past I've noticed that once there's been a bit of commotion in the swim the carp will move off, and you might as well go home. I'd suggest having one rod half way and your other rod 20 yards out!

I've always looked under bridges, thinking the carp must like it under there, but on the whole of my local canal I can only think of one bridge that produces carp, but this bridge is unused. Once again I think this is more because the carp spook off from the noise and vibrations. I mean who wants to eat below a bridge with cars going over your head? The other issue fishing under bridges is that things often get chucked off them, so you never know what you're fishing over! When it comes to narrowboats, some carp will associate these boats with food, as scraps of food get chucked over the side! Unfortunately some canal authorities' rules restricted you from fishing in the areas the boats are moored. If this is the case I'd suggest fishing as close to the area as you can and baiting a line from the boats to your spot. Another good way I've found fishing near narrowboats it to float bread on the top. But before I do that I would cast out two over-depth zigs with fake bread downwind from the carp. As long as the wind's pushing the right direction you can lure the carp away from the boats into the area your zigs are. Be warned though, doing this can result in multiple takes! On my local canals there are a few lakes which branch off from the canal. These lakes are fenced off and used as fisheries or private grounds. You will find that the fences never go all the way down, normally leaving about two to three foot allowing fish to move in and out of the canal. These areas are where the monsters live, and every now and then they move into the canal and get caught.

Now once you've found the areas you are planning on fishing it's well worthwhile looking at the gear you're going to need to take with you. Fishing with everything including the kitchen sink is definitely not the way forward; you need to be as light as you can, as in canals and small narrow dark areas, having a 12ft rod can be a nightmare. Ideally you need a 9ft 3lb rod. This may seem overkill, but don't underestimate the power of carp in a small canal, as they have nowhere to go. I have a set of Wychwood Extractors; these small, tough rods are the only ones for me. They come in a 6ft version too, and this is ideal for under bridges! When it comes to reel choice, the Shimano ST Baitrunners are the ones for me. There is absolutely no need for a big pit on the canal; they're too bulky and will get in the way. Being a tackle tart on the canal will just end up with disaster. The amount of times I have cyclist running over my rods and dogs chewing my cork handle, and yes this really does happen! I've had rods go for swims during the night when a barge has decided to come past and ignore the fact that my Delkims are screaming! This is why I always use back leads. This eliminates any problems with boats. When I decide to spend the night

Split Tail from the Basingstoke canal at 40lb 2oz.

My local tackle shop where the tales from the canals are recited.

What a stunner! The big common at 35lb 6oz.

Ash Vale Flash in Aldershot.

Tackle and equipment – Colnmere baiting spoon.

Set up ready for action.

The float will drop or move when a fish is on your area.

The blackberries blend in nicely with the hemp.

down the canal I use a little 60-inch brolly system, as there's not a lot of room on the public footpaths, and to be honest spending more than 24 hours at the canal is extremely hard, as the only thing you're looking at is 15 yards of water. For the anglers moving on from big gravel pits this can be a challenge in itself.

Weed rakes can be really handy on canals, not so much clearing weed but cleaning the bottom of debris. The one pictured has a 30ft rope attached, so it easily drags back most items including the odd bike or trolley! Once I've cleared the area with the rake, I'll put my waders on and check the area myself to make sure I know what I'm fishing over! I wouldn't suggest doing this on your own though – always have a friend with you and take a prodding stick to check your next step, and never go in the water if there's boat traffic of any kind! ! This is an advantage in a lot of different ways: not only can you tell what the bottom is made up of, but you can also see depths and the colour of the bottom. Another good tip is to trim a little hole in the overhanging trees as long as it's not an SSSI area. (Site of Special Scientific Interest).

Now I've known people to make their own gravel spots after they've done this. I'm not saying go buy tons of gravel and fill it in, but a 25kg sack of pea shingle should be more than enough to make a decent hard area for you to fish over! Just make sure you give the shingle a good clean before you chuck it into the canal. If the canal authority has a problem with this, you can always use Sensas gravel, which match anglers use to make their groundbait sink faster. It's basically gravel, but as it's designed to be used with bait they shouldn't have a problem with it. When it comes to baiting up or putting your rig over your area, the Colnemere Developments bait pole is the only way forward. This will allow you to bait up and place your rig easily and quietly in the day or night. It comes with a standard reach of 12 meters, which is more than enough for most canals, but you can buy extra 1.8m infinite extensions, allowing you to reach those spots next to the boats in the turning bays or the moorings, not to mention getting under those overhanging trees on the far bank where carp always seem to be. I also use the pole when prebaiting; it's a fast way to get a lot of bait out, as the spoon can hold well over a kilo of mixed feed, making it the stealthiest form of prebaiting you can do.

Another piece of tackle that is extremely handy is a pole rig. My idea behind this is to place the pole rig over my baited area permanently fixed to the canal bed. This will stay out there until I have finished my session. This will help you see if there are any fish over your spot. The pole float will move when a carp swims underneath it, giving you a heads up when the fish are over your spot!

Canal fish, like all carp, eat anything and everything, but I've found some carp do have their favorite snacks! If you look close enough whilst you walk down the canal you will find loads of natural food that the carp love! At the right time of year blackberries have got to be one of the best; they have a sweet, sharp taste that the carp seem to love! This has to be one of my favorite baits; not only is it free, but when the berries get knocked off by the birds it naturally prebaits the swim! The blackberries can also be great for adding to a stick mix or to coat boilies with. Once in the water it gives off a nice halo of attractions. Be aware though, some of the berries can float, so it's worth sticking them into a bucket of water first and using the floaters as an extra in your stick mix.

Sweetcorn is another effective bait, as match and pleasure anglers use this frequently so it forms part of their diet all year round. The downside of sweetcorn is that because of the colour you may find unwelcome attention from the ducks or a swim full of bream, but don't let this put you off, as most of the carp I have caught from the canal have been using the Evo corn stacks as a hook bait. Another free bait you can collect and use on the canal are crayfish. The carp love these. I tend to crush them up and add them to my boilie mix or cook them and use the meat in a stick mix. I believe this will give you an edge any time of year, but please remember to only use the crayfish on the area of the canal you caught them, as you can end up spreading crayfish eggs on parts of the canal that haven't got a large number of crayfish in.

When it comes to selecting a boilie anything works, but using fishmeals or bright boilies can be tricky, as almost straight away the crayfish will be tucking into your bait. I use a dark milk protein boilie or a good quality bloodworm based boilie. I don't think the size of boilies matter at all at the canal, but if you do have a lot of bream in your swim I'd suggest 20mm. The smaller fish will still have a go at the boilies, as I've seen on my underwater cameras. I've seen roach lift 18mm boilies clean off the deck! Now we all see bloodworm in today's baits, but how much bloodworm is actually used in creating the bait? Apart from a few top brands there's not as much as you might think, and most of the bloodworm that get added is in powder form, not fresh. I buy the 1kg Marine Nutrition 100% Bloodworm, and as this is same price as a kilo of boilies it's great value for the money. The carp will feed over this all year round, and I've found it to be the best bait to keep all the pests away on the canal.

They also do 1kg bags of Mysis. This tiny freshwater shrimp has a very high nutritional profile, and the carp simply can't get enough of the stuff. The only downside to these baits is that it can tend to go off on the bank in the warmer months. You can stop this by adding salt and water. By doing this in the right levels you can drain the excess water away in a sieve, and you have PVA-friendly 100% pure bloodworm Mysis. These little bags are ideal for stalking; when I've used this method in the past I've found that tipping the Evolution corn stacks with a maggot cluster blends into the bloodworm providing a stealthy hookbait. Liquid additive is a funny one really; personally I don't add anything apart from hemp oil or Betalin to my baits or hookbaits. I think you can end up making the bait too obvious to the carp. I aim for a nice balance but long-lasting additives.

Once you've found the carp on the canal it's always worthwhile starting to prebait. I would start by baiting up with sweetcorn, as this is probably the most introduced bait. A tin each day for a week would be a good start. This will help you out later on matching your plastic sweetcorn hookbait. This will also keep the crays away for longer. After the first week I would check my spot for activity and remaining bait! How is this possible without disturbing the fish, you might ask? The Waterwolf underwater camera is the way forward. This cheap little camera will drop to the bottom showing any bait left in the swim, and with its massive four-and-a-half hour recording time, on day seven it's worth leaving the camera out to check which fish are coming into your swim! A few days after the capture of Split Tail, I decided to drop the camera in to see how much of the bait

Bloodworms in the purest form fished with bloodworm boilies – a lethal mix!

My trusty Waterwolf. It's amazing what's on the market these days.

The dark 22lb mirror.

Evolution corn stacks.

The D-rig with a Cell wafter, perfectly balanced.

The deadly 360-rig.

Cracker at 38lb

Arthur, named as he has half a tail, 31lb 2oz.

had gone. I left it out here for a few hours just in case I got footage of any carp feeding, and when I plugged it into the laptop that's exactly what I saw. This was enough for me to get my rods out of the car and fish for a few hours, and sure enough an hour after placing my rig out I had this beautiful 22lb dark mirror!

If you don't have the camera, spending an evening watching the water may not be as effective, but will still give you an idea if the fish are feeding. Depending on what you find you may wish to fish the swim, but don't rush into it. The more time the fish feed in one area the more chance you have of seeing new carp in the swim, as canal carp tend to stick together in pairs or small shoals. Once you have a few fish in your area, I wouldn't think twice about starting to add boilies to the mix. The size of the fish and amount of fish will determine how much you decide to put in. When I was fishing for Split Tail from the Basingstoke, I was using anything from 1kg to 5kg of boilies a week, and when the fish were feeding hard I was feeding them 5kg of mixed chops a day along with a tin of corn. What most people

27lb.

forget is that the canals are full of pest fish, and I've seen little roach and rudd on the underwater camera, smashing into the boilies, so how many pest fish you have will also determine the amount of smaller baits you decide to use.

As a rule I would leave the swim for at least two weeks before I start to fish. This allows the carp to feed freely, and in return for your efforts you should have a fish on your first session. Another way I've found very effective on the canal is to tie PVA bags full of little goodies to chuck in whilst on my walks. I would spend my spare time in the evenings tying these up ready for the next day. I'd make up anything up to 50 bags a night, and as I was at home I even got the missus involved! Prebaiting can be very expensive, so if you're on a budget I'd look at cooking up your own particles, sticking with mainly hemp and maize, but be sensible and prepare it properly. Also you can use the blackberries I mentioned earlier; you can find tons of these on canals, and they won't cost you a thing! Mashing them up and mixing them with liquidised bread will create a nice bed of bait that the carp will be more than happy to feed over.

Now when I think about what rigs I would use on canals, the first thing that comes to mind is all the rubbish on the bottom, the silt and the crayfish, so straight away all my hook links are at least ten inches long. Then I start looking at what hook link material I use. I normally fish with 12lb fluorocarbon; in my opinion the clear material is bombproof, but with all these obstacles I still increase that to 15lb fluoro, and in extreme cases I will use a 30lb coated braid. Now this may make you laugh or make you think twice about carp fishing, but I always use the biggest hooks I can get my hands on. I take this approach in all my angling, but it's even more effective on the canal, as the carp tend to have really tough mouths from eating all the crayfish. The Krank in size 2 is my preferred hook pattern, but I have used Continental Muggers in the same size. You may tie the rig of your choice with the hooks and think to yourself it looks silly and it's overkill, but over the last few years it's all I've used, and yes, in my option it has increased my catch rate massively. It's also reducing the amount of hook pulls; I would say 99% of the fish I have hooked I have landed, and I put this all down to the size of the hooks.

The main question I get asked is what about the smaller carp? Surely they will notice the hook when taking the bait. This brings me onto the next part of all my rigs – critically balanced hookbaits. If used in the right way these little gems will act natural in the water, and fish will fed confidently around the bait, and you will nail the first fish that picks it up. An 18mm Cell wafter will be critically balanced on a size two Krank. There's no need for putty – one less thing to worry about. The same can be said for the Evolution corn stacks, these deadly little pop-up corn will sit perfectly above a size 2, and as they're plastic they will withstand the battering of the crayfish! I've caught all sizes of carp on size 2 hooks from the smallest at 7lb right up to 46lb, not to mention this was the rig that caught me Split Tail!

Now I'll move onto types of rigs I would and wouldn't use. I'll start off with the chod rig that I refuse to use whilst fishing on a the canal, as the 'chuck it and hope' is not my kind of angling. I'm more precise and would rather not fish than chuck something out I'm not 100% confident in. The hinge stiff rig is another one that personally I wouldn't use, as I prefer to use a stiff boom section, and you simply can't use that on my local canal, as the rig won't sit right with all the debris. The KD rig is another no-go for me, as there are too many pests, and the hair can end up twisted around the shank, making the rig useless. I've found the basic blowback rigs and hair rigs all do well when on the canal, but I have more confidence using the D-rig; this simple rig is so effective. I've stalked carp and seen the carp hooked on the first time the fish has attempted to suck the bait into its mouth. The most important part of this rig is the amount of turns on the whipping knot and the amount of turns on the knotless knot. I use seven turns on the whip and five turns on the knotless. Combined with the critically-balanced hookbait, this will allow the hookpoint to be heavier than the eye, allowing the point to drop and take hold. A very important part of the rig is to ensure the top whipping knot is in line with the barb, or where the barb should be on a barbless hook. Using a micro ring hook swivel will give you the added movement on the hook bait as well as letting it move freely over the fluorocarbon. I tend to use this rig along with two metres of tubing. This might sound overkill, but it keeps your line pinned down and protected when you're playing the fish. Anyway it's not like you've got to worry about casting far.

Let's move on to the 360-rig, another effective rig for the canal, as the rig will sit on anything that's on the bottom. The 360-rig is very unpredictable as far as hook holds are concerned. I've found using the Fox longshank curve to be the best hook pattern to combat this problem. Another problem you may find with this rig is that in recent years the rig has been banned from venues, as the eye of the hook can get caught up in landing nets and rip the carp's mouths. A away to combat this is by covering the eye with a small piece of shrink tube. This will stop the eye getting caught up when the fish has been landed. Tying the rig couldn't be more simple: the only knots that are involved are four-turn grinner knots on each side of the swivels. I would start by threading a size 11 ring swivel onto a size 8 Fox long shanked curved hook. This will give the hook the weight and movement. I would then place my first hook bead right the way down the shank, locking the swivel down to the eye of the hook.

The next component is a critical part of the rig – the Thinking Anglers micro ringed hook swivel. This amazing piece of tackle will provide the right amount of movement for the hookbait whilst on the shank. To finish off the hook you simply add one more hook bead opposite the barb to lock the hook swivel into place. I would then tie a semi-soft boom section like IQ2 from the hook to my cog system, and that simply, it's job done. Now when it comes to hookbaits you need just the right balance; the hook needs to sit up right from the ring swivel. This can be done by simply using the Evolution corn stacks. If you would like to use pop-ups then I suggest adding putty just under the rig swivel.

The last piece of advice I can give you is to work closely with other anglers and respect each other's views. I can think of two anglers on the Basingstoke canal I hold in high regard and have a well desevered mention in this piece. If it wasn't for Cameron Coxhead I wouldn't have any photos of Split Tail. On the day of the capture I had no camera other than my phone, but within ten minutes of landing the specimen, Cameron was there on the bank carrying a camera with a set of spare scales and willing to strip down to his boxers to take water shots for me. That's sportsmanship at its finest, my friends. He was rewarded with this fine specimen called Cracker weighing in at 38lb – another example of angling at its finest.

Now the other chap, Will Crowdy, is a pure carp catching machine. He was a carp in his previous life! He's the only angler I know who would rather eat boilies than a Pot Noodle – a pure book of knowledge. This young chap kept me up to date with the canal whilst I was out of the country, and when I returned the three of us worked together for weeks, keeping each other updated on the swims and fish activity. Canals are all about working as a team; even if you have your own separate spots it's always handy to have a mate pop down to see what's happening in your swim. Here he is with Arthur at 31lb 2oz, another old fish.

I hope you have enjoyed reading this as much as I have enjoyed writing it. Hopefully the future of our canals in Britain will be full of great angling events such as the ones I have written about. It would mean a lot to me to see more anglers fishing the canals protecting the fish from being either removed or eaten. I'll leave you with this thought: if I canal carp can grow to over 40lbs who's to say there's not a fifty in your local? I know there's bigger carp in mine.

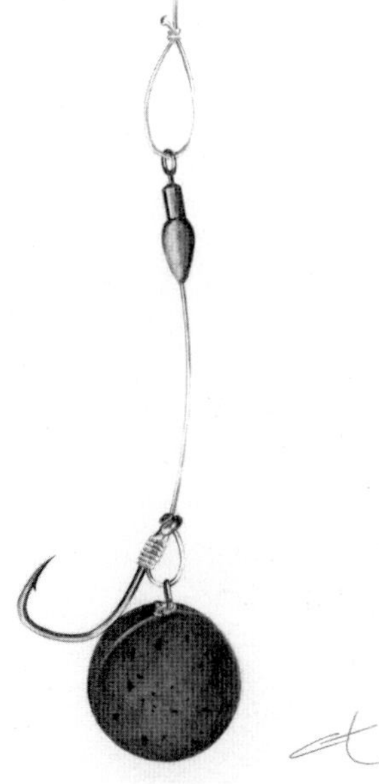

Chapter 2

The Royal Military Canal

A Tale Of Two Records

By Bill Phillips

The ripple rings ebbed away from the yellow blob bobbing in the middle. A young boy sat trembling with excitement gazing at a bright yellow grayling float, willing it to disappear. Dreams of the culprit being a monster of the deeps, swallowing his dough paste bait, are suddenly interrupted by the reality of the strike. Splish splash and a pristine little gudgeon is swung ashore. The elation felt was unforgettable, I was now a fisherman. It was a truly defining moment in my life.

That is my first memory of fishing a canal; I was alone and happy in my own company. It was on the Grand Union somewhere near Tring. My tackle was a length of cane, some cord, and, compliments of a step Uncle, a proper float with a hook to gut.

I had fished farm ponds many times using a cork for float and bent pin for the hook, and the result of this was lots of bites but never any fish. When the bent pin was replaced by a hook I caught loads of small roach and rudd. On the advice of Uncle Albert I tried smaller hooks, which resulted in lots more fish. He also told me to try worm as bait, which I did on my next canal visit. The result was what seemed at the time, a massive perch. Two very important basic lessons learned.

Step Uncle Albert was a bit of an odd character but a keen angler. He never took me fishing but would utter advice and allowed me to look in his tackle shed. I would spend hours in that shed, looking at all the cane rods, drum reels, nets and line on rollers. I must confess that I did sneak a few old floats, hooks and sinkers into my pocket. He confided in me that he was interested in carp, which he fished for with potatoes.

I was given a home-made bamboo rod with an old wooden reel. Armed with such gear I decided to catch a carp. Many hours were spent on both the ponds and the canal with chunks of a raw King Edward potato on the hook. Needless to say, I soon gave up, but not before another lesson was learned. It was on the canal again, and as usual I was catching nothing on the spud, and changing to dough paste was marginally better. A passing stranger saw me eating a cheese sandwich and said, “Put a bit of that cheese on the hook son; you’ll catch roach.” He was right: as soon as I changed to cheese I caught several decent roach. The importance of the right bait was becoming apparent.

My life as a child was a bit of a mess to say the least. I lost my mother when I was nine. My “father” was an evil man and abused me terribly. He was a farm worker that changed jobs at least a couple of times a year, which meant we kept moving from one area to another. Schooling was impossible, so my outlet became fishing, I would go whenever I could.

By the time I was about twelve we were living in Kent, not too far from the Royal Military Canal, a water that over the years was to influence my fishing, and indeed my life a great deal. The RMC is deep in the south east of England. It stretches for about 25 miles from Iden lock in the west, eastward through the Romney marshes to Shorncliffe sluice. It is not navigable so there was no boat traffic other than an odd canoe.

At twelve years old all fishing was magical; nothing was too much trouble for the reward of a few hours’ fishing. The canal was about seven miles from home so accessible by push bike. Rods tied to the cross-bar with binder twine, a wicker basket on my back, and most weekends and holidays would see me pedaling frantically towards the canal. The journey took me from the main A20, along Otterpool Lane and past Lymne Airport. Then the highlight, the descent of Lymne Hill, a steep, long and in hindsight, very dangerous. Often, I would be with fishing mate Steve. We would set ourselves at the top, as if on a starting grid, and then race like lunatics to the bottom. The prize to the winner was first choice of swims. Unfortunately, it occasionally resulted in parting company with bikes causing injuries and tackle damage. Stupid, but we still did it, and miraculously we never really got hurt. Probably the worst pain was at the end of a long day’s fishing, weighted down with tackle, the half hour or so pushing the bikes back up that wretched hill.

The section of the RMC that ran along the bottom of the hill was known as West Hythe, it was controlled by Cinque Ports Club. The main reason for fishing there was because it was the closest to home. The water was shallow, weedy and murky. In those oh so magic days, nothing seemed to matter. There was always the feeling of anticipation that we would catch a monster. We never did of course, but the enthusiasm was relentless.

My tackle now consisted of bamboo rods with Intrepid Black Prince and Regent reels. Favourite floats were of the grayling type. I'm sure that was due to the rings of ripples they produced when signalling a bite. Occasionally, a really good bite would be heard as the float "plopped" under. What a lovely sound that was! We often caught lots of small roach, bream, perch, occasionally a tench and then pike in the winter. Never, in those days did we catch carp. We knew of them, but had read, heard and believed that they were all but uncatchable. Even to talk about them had to be done in a slow whisper. It is so strange now to reflect on the mystery the word "carp" portrayed. Very occasionally, monster carp would be seen, usually drifting under the old brick road bridge, which was so often a vantage point to be fished from.

It must have been about 1962 when I was first infected by the carp virus. I didn't know it at the time, but it was a massive influence on the future of my life's fishing. The day was hot and still; I was fishing alone at West Hythe and was bored with the lack of action in the heat of the midday sun. On the opposite bank I became aware of a presence, an almost ghostlike figure, crouched between two elder bushes. He was obviously fishing, but what a daft place to fish, I remember thinking. Eventually, curiosity got the better of me and I went round to have a closer look. As I approached from the bank above him, I could smell his pipe. It was gently puffing clouds of grey smoke that hovered around him like a mist. "What are you doing mister?" I asked. "Carp, lad. Carp," was the slow, determined answer. He somehow produced an air that made me sit low and quiet, also like a magnetic field that would not release me. I sat and studied. His tackle was simple, but it looked strong. Where was his float? All I could see was some chunks of bread in the marginal lilies to his right. Now and again he would slowly lift his finger, point and whisper, "There." This confused me, but I did not ask; I just nodded knowingly.

Gradually, over the weeks of that summer, I got to know a little about this strange fellow. His name was Ron, and he was fishing floating crust for carp. Only once did I see him catch; it was a common carp of some six pounds. This virtual stranger, and the awesome fish I saw him land had a deep and lasting impression. I was infected for life, and in fact became a carrier of the incurable carp fever. I often wonder if he knew, or if he is even still alive.

The virus lay semi-dormant for several years while I served a long, enjoyable apprenticeship acquiring the skills in the art of angling. During this time, the memory of Ron and his carp would often haunt me. I knew that one day, when ready, I would also catch a monster carp.

Some readers of this magazine are probably thinking, "Whatever has

My first canal 20 at 22lb 8oz back in 1973.

The smaller of the two 'dug out' swims.

The only time in my life I will ever catch my first canal carp, 17th June, 1973.

June 1973, 22lb 8oz – a turning point in my fishing career.

Swim preparation to clear the pads.

August 1974, a new PB and AAC record at 25lb 7oz.

The 'plopping' of pads is a definite sign of carp.

A typical early canal catch laid out on the dreaded hessian sack.

this all got to do with big carp fishing?" I make no apology for this. It is to try and give modern day carpers an insight into the apprenticeship that we old school carp anglers served. Virtually no carp tackle or bait was commercially available as it is today. We had to be innovative, resourceful and to a degree pioneering. We all contributed to making the world of carp fishing what it is today, available to all.

Marriage, children, career, and creating a home took priority during my late teens until 1969/70. 1969 was a watershed. My home and work was now in Ashford. I had been fishing a beautiful stretch of the Royal Military Canal at Aldergate, mainly for tench, but I had seen carp. Ashford Angling Club had control of the fishing between Iden lock and West Hythe dam, some fifteen or so miles. This was my favoured stretch of water, full of character and very pretty. This is where it all really began.

A love affair resulting in a marriage that lasted a decade is probably the best way to describe my passion for the RMC in the 1970s. Even now, forty five years on I still get very emotional when I reflect. Sadness for the loss of that irretrievable magic but then joy for the privilege to have experienced such a personal passionate relationship with such a wonderful water. Strangely, as if it were yesterday, I can smell the water, the grass, the trees and even that 'fishy' scent that only the habitual angler can understand. The relentless croaking of the frogs at dawn, the chatting of the birds as they seek their evening roost, all coupled with the roar of the lions as they are fed at nearby Port Lymne Wildlife Park. Recollections of the slightest flickering of the lily pads causing ripples around individual pads, the occasional light plop as a pad is submerged, clearly showing the presence of a carp. Oh what wonderful memories.

Alas, so much has now changed. The romance and mystery has long gone. A change of controlling clubs has allowed a large part of it to fall into disrepair. But, who knows, maybe she still holds a few treasures; if I still lived in Kent I would certainly be looking. However, here are a few stories from those magical years in the seventies, a time when many carp anglers were truly habitual, striving against all odds. They rose to the challenges, solved the mysteries, enjoyed their failures and were ecstatic with any level of success.

Aldergate is between Giggers Green bridge and West Hythe dam, a distance of three to four miles without the interruption of a road bridge. This made it the most secluded and undisturbed length of the canal. It was the middle reaches of Aldergate, the farthest walk from the bridges where I was to start my campaign to catch a canal carp on the magical 16th June 1970. I had discovered the consistent presence of my intended quarry in this most beautiful area. It's a magnificent stretch of water, and to this day, my absolute favourite, with open fields to the south, nestled into the base of a steep hillside to the north. Bedded into the hillside was Port Lymne Wildlife Park and its noises, the ruins of Stutfall Castle and Lymne Castle. All added to the eeriness when fishing alone as darkness fell. No fishing was allowed from the north bank. It was mostly thick with trees, many of which overhung the water. High heavy bullrushes in much of the margins completed the backdrop. During the summer the water was fairly clear with depths of three feet in the margins, shelving to eight feet in the centre. The average width of about fifty feet was largely occupied by twenty feet wide margins of lesser yellow water lilies on both banks. Most anglers hated them, but both the carp and I loved them.

Over the next three years I spent nearly 700 hours failing to catch a single carp but did hook and lose a few. Some of my efforts were so obscure by today's standards. Rubber gloves, wooden deck chair, Fairy Liquid tops and candles in jam jars. I even went through a stage of preconditioning tinned potatoes in the canal for a few days to impregnate them with water bugs before I would use them on the hook. This was after only ever getting takes on potatoes that had been out for over 24 hours. Floating crust in the margins was one of my more conventional and nearly successful methods.

By 1973 I had built up a considerable knowledge of both the water and the carp. I knew most were commons to mid teens with a few bigger mirrors that I saw often. The close season was spent preparing a couple of swims in the remote Aldergate area where the banks were high and steep making fishing at night difficult. To overcome this, I dug the bank out to allow my deckchair and tackle to fit in a nice flat pitch just above water level. Sheep hurdles were laid over the top of the dugouts followed by sacking and turf so as to obscure the cave-like den beneath. Rushes were planted in the front of the swim to obscure the presence of yours truly. Tinned potatoes and bread were introduced for a couple of weeks prior to the start of the season. Signs were put up with the words "Pre-baited swim. Please do not fish. Bill Phillips." No one ever did, such was the level of honour. Can you imagine doing that these days? Over the following few years the bigger swim was encroached by a family of badgers and became a set for a couple of decades. Those badgers, along with many other wild creatures, became a fascinating part of my time on the canal.

The start of the 1973/4 season was the turning point in my canal carp fishing career. I not only caught my first RMC carp but also had one of the big mirrors. I arrived on the opening night equipped with the right tools for the job: a Richard Walker Mk 1V, Mitchell 314 reel and Heron alarms. The bait was to be my conditioned potatoes on a size 4 hook free-lined on 8lb line. The first night was uneventful. I had to work in the morning but returned at 11pm. During that night I lost two carp, one of which pulled the rod in and broke the line. At first light a fast take followed by a short but lively fight, resulted in the landing of my first ever RMC carp, a small common weighing 4lb 12oz. I don't expect anyone reading to understand how much that small fish meant to me. My duck was broken. This was the only time in my life I would ever catch my first canal carp.

At 8am I had another take, and I was into a much bigger fish. Thirty yards of line were ripped from the reel as it ran for an overhanging tree opposite. After several more runs, a few problems with weed and getting it in the net, somehow I managed to get it on the bank. It was a magnificent 22lb 8oz leather carp. Later it was officially weighed and recorded as a record for Ashford AC. To say I was elated is an understatement; I was now a carp angler. Surely the marriage was born out of the love affair with this wonderful water. On reflection, that night was to remain one the most action packed nights I was ever to have on the RMC. The remainder of that season, although eventful in many ways only produced another three carp in 250 hours. I never stopped enjoying the magic of the challenge, and even though I had other easier waters to fish, I rarely betrayed the water I had grown so fond of. The harder a thing is to achieve, the greater the satisfaction, and that I am sure was the driving force.

The 1974/5 season was to be my most successful in terms of numbers with nine carp up to a new PB and Ashford club record of 25lb 7oz. However, I did spend a lot more time there, recording 500 hours. During that time I recorded many wildlife events of interest. Badgers and foxes became friends, and encounters could be startling to say the least. My diary reads "Almost kissed a fox."

Picture this: It was a warm, still August night, and I was fishing alone in the big dugout. There was an eerie feel to the night; it was very dark and felt stormy. The roof of the dugout had gone so a brolly was erected to form a roof, which was about level with the top of the bank behind me. The roar of the lions from the wildlife park was louder than usual. I had goosebumps, and the hairs on the back of my neck stood up, an uneasy sort of feeling to say the least. I shrank back in my deckchair, watching the bottle top indicators in the flickering candlelight. My eyes began to close, and I started to drift when I became aware of a presence. Very, very slowly the brolly started to turn. There was virtually no sound as it continued to sway gently around. I absolutely froze, too frightened to move or look. God knows what I thought it was, but I know I nearly gave birth. After what seemed an age, I plucked up the courage to turn around and look. By this time the brolly had tilted over. My head was about level with the top of the bank, as I peered over the edge of the dugout, I literally came nose to nose with the culprit. We both momentarily stopped and stared into each other's eyes. Then, all hell let loose. I jumped up, knocking everything flying. The fox gave a high pitched yelp and did a wheelspin as it bolted off, actually kicking dirt in my face. There I was, heart thumping, shaking, but at the same time laughing.

In 1974/5 a family of badgers took up residence in the big dugout and really made a mess of it. They became part of every fishing session on the canal and belong as much in my memory as the carp themselves. Over the years, they often startled me or spooked the fish, but always fascinated me and eventually became less shy. They even started taking bits of sandwiches and bait. They can, at times, be fairly aggressive. My poor old dog, Patches, a fishing companion in the later years, was absolutely petrified of them. When he heard them snorting about in the night he would hide under the

32lb, RMC, 28th October, 1978.

30 inches to 'V' of tail and 29.5 inches girth.

32lb, 28th October 1978.

Ashford's keen carp angler Bill Phillips has had his 32lb carp taken from his club's canal waters at Aldergate recognised as a British

He has been building up to this big catch having taken 20 pound - plus carps from canals twice before, with a 22lb 8oz one in 1973 and a 25lb

Canal record 32lb in 1978.

way they can differentiate between this and any other bait smelling of P.Y.M., so if some-one has baited with P.Y.M. made up with dry casein the fish are almost certain to reject your bait. If you bait up with good bait such as 2 P.Y.M., 5 casein, 2 soya flour, 1 gluten, which is aprox. 69% protein, and then someone else begins to fish with a lower value bait made with P.Y.M. they will be making use of your baiting and will in fact catch fish which think they are taking your bait, if they bait up heavily with a lower P.Y.M. bait, say a 50% protein bait it will mean your results will not be as good as they should be, while they will catch more fish than their baiting deserves.

Personally my advice would be, if in doubt don't use P.Y.M. at all, but instead go for an Equivite bait with a flavour or smell added to it. For instance 1 equivite, 6 casein, 2 soya flour, 1 gluten, + smell, this would be aprox 70% protein. In fact it is these type of baits that I have concentrated on for the last few years, since P.Y.M. became widely known. Whichever type you choose to use, the method of making up the baits is the same.

For bottom baits mix up the ten ounces of dry material, beat up 6 standard eggs and mix it all together. Roll into balls and put into boiling water for about 1 minute (the actual length of time will decide the strength of the skin) strain and dry. I use a

Fred Wilton's letter advising on bait recipes for the canal.

Small pound backwater on the K and A. Some of these areas are very 'carpy'.

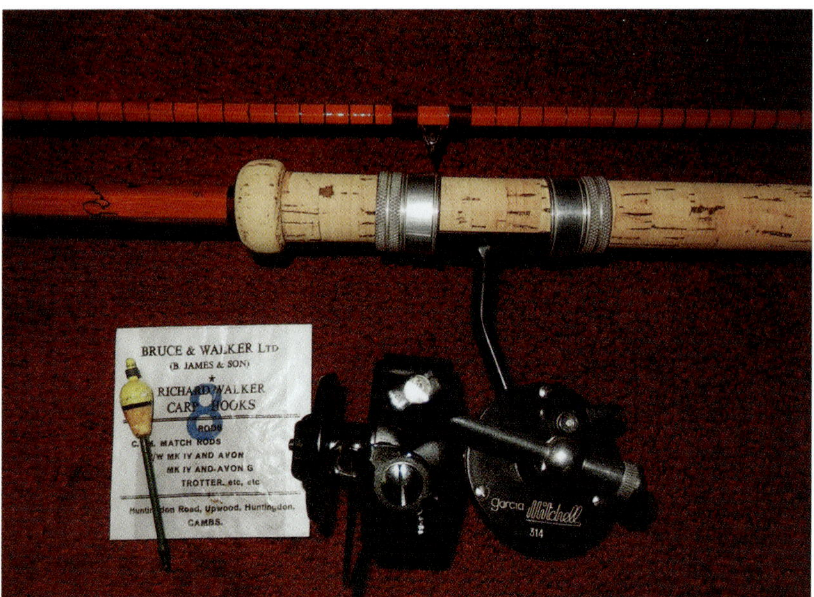

My original old canal carp fishing armoury: Richard Walker Mk IV rod, Michell 314 reel, RW hooks and the grayling float I used as a boy.

The hessian sack catastrophe that now hangs on my study wall.

The Hague Canal in Holland was a fascinating place to fish.

The Holiday Cottage pound before the boat traffic got too heavy.

bedchair, shaking like a leaf. I don't know whether it's a descendant of the same family or not, but the badger set, as the swim became known, was still there when I last visited some 35 years on and may well still be there today.

I could go on about the canal's wildlife, but guess I had better return to the fishing. Or is it one and the same thing? One big catastrophe of the 1974 summer was the loss of a lovely 10¾lb common whilst being retained in a sack. It was a gloriously hot and still August day. The previous night had been uneventful so I reeled in to go stalking. There were a few carp basking in the lilies but not interested in my floating crust bait. Then I spotted movement in a bed of lilies close in. No fish were to be seen but the plopping and humping of the pads were definite signs of a carp feeding on snails beneath them. Lying in the grass I very gently lowered a small piece of crust where I thought its nose may be. In an instant the crust was gone, and I was into one of the hardest fighting canal carp I had ever had. The line cut through the lilies like a scythe as it made run after run. After at least twenty minutes I was so pleased when it rolled into the net. On my return to the swim for weighing and photographing, I realised the camera had been left at home. I desperately wanted a picture so decided to sack it and go home for the camera. Back then, the sacks we used were the old hessian grain sacks that we were to later realise did not allow enough water exchange.

Anyway, I am sure you have by now guessed that on my return the poor fish was dead, having spent several hours, in the heat of the day, starved of oxygen. I was devastated.

However, it did encourage me to me to make some lightweight sacks from tent material for future sackings. Lots of small holes were punched in for good circulation, and a proper drawstring was attached. It was another one of those big lessons that were learned along the way.

Not knowing what to do with the dead fish and worried that I might be in trouble if anyone found out, I wrapped it in the sack and took it home to bury. While at home I made a few inquiries and found a fairly local taxidermist who quoted £23 to set it up in a glass case for me. Even though it was a great deal of money I could ill afford at the time, I decided to have it done rather than just bury it. That lovely common now hangs on my study wall among a collection of old fish taxidermy and memorabilia that it is largely responsible for.

The 1976/7 season saw me accepted to the BCSG and learning from other carp anglers. One of the members that vetted me was Fred Wilton. Fred was kind enough to write me a letter with bait formulations to try on the canal. That season I did my biggest baiting campaign ever on the canal, and it resulted in my most frustrating seasons. I even purchased a small motorbike to use for travelling the 20-mile round trip to bait up every few days from April to June 16th. The bait was a PYM protein boiled bait with a floater made with the same mix. As an alternative I also baited with broad beans. I even tied dozens of broad beans to short lengths of line, attached them to stones and threw them in, the idea being that the carp would get used to tacking them with line attached and feel safe. Well, the eels went mad for the PYM, even in floater form. The couple of carp I did hook on the PYM were stalked, but both lost. Broad beans, in spite of being very successful on other waters, only produced bite-offs, which indicated my confidence building with the line had worked. Also they caught loads of tench and bream on the canal. In short the bait had worked so well for other species, the carp didn't get a look in. By September I had spent nearly 400 hours and not landed a single carp.

My confidence was waning, and I was doing fewer hours. Mid-September and I was wandering the bank around Aldergate while waiting for a mate to go to another venue. All I had with me was a rod, net and loaf of bread. I soon spotted a carp tight to the far bank. Bread would not coax it to take so I decided to find a worm to try. The fish appeared to be feeding from a slight inflow caused by the recent rain. With only free-line available I used mud around the hook and worm for weight to enable a cast onto the far bank, so as not to spook the fish. Wonders will never cease- it worked first time. A couple of sharp tugs on the line and there it was, a nice free-lined worm in the opposite margin. A few moments later and the carp was on. Only a small common at 9lb 4oz, but I was as pleased with that fish as I would have been with a big twenty from any other water, probably more so.

The capture of that small common was a turning point in my RMC fishing. I still wanted to catch canal carp but in less hours and less cost. I reasoned that hundreds of rod hours resulted in a lot of blanks. Short sessions after time spent looking for fish often resulted in success. I decided to try and catch carp in fewer hours by the use of thorough observation. A method that is known to be successful but not often practised. The chart below was a good reason to give it a try.

Observation fishing on the RMC certainly paid dividends in the seasons that followed. That allowed me to do a lot more on other waters while still catching a few canal fish. In 1977, observation plus only 25 hours' fishing produced the same result that the 400 hours the year before.

My approach to the RMC for the 1978 season was to be the same. Observation first, and only when fish were found would a line be cast. Closed season visits resulted in only a few small commons being seen. I decided to leave it for the early part of the season enabling me to fish elsewhere and give the canal a rest. I would still spend a few evenings a month looking for some better fish. During each visit, I would put in a few of my latest super bait that was taking the Kent carp apart, "Robin Red".

STATISTICS FOR THAT 1976 SEASON – £ Cost, rate at the time:

Item	Cost
Miles travelled = 1,364	£34.10
Hours fishing = 400	£800.00
Tackle breakage	£20.00
broad beans = 336 tins	£28.00
PYM dry mix = 12lb	£17.00
Eggs = 228	£8.50
Worms = 1	No charge

Carp caught = 1 at 9lb 4oz
Cost of Carp = £6.13 per ounce.
Mental state of angler = IN QUESTION.

It was not until late October that a couple of big carp were located. Then and only then did I do a few short sessions. 28th October saw me creeping the banks on a beautiful warm sunny afternoon. My armoury was a 10ft RW glass rod with 14lb line to combat the decaying weed and branches, rod rest, landing net, a sack (just in case), bread and some Robin Red paste. After a while I found a big mirror in the margins. I crawled through the bushes and watched for a while. What a fantastic sight it was too, with magnificent clear water, a monster carp in full view, picking at the odd leaf on the surface looking very catchable. Very gently I presented a small piece of crust. A few nervous moments passed, and it swam close to the crust, stopped, flicked its fins and swam away. That fish was undoubtedly disturbed by the presence of my crust.

Dragging my net away from the bushes with some force, whilst trying to watch that departing carp, I set off in pursuit, but lost sight of it. Consolation was found in the location of a very big common grubbing about in gin-clear water. A small piece of paste was flicked past the fish and drawn back in its path. Unfortunately, whilst trying to gain the last few inches, my bait caught on a stem and came off. Unable to move, I could not rebait without spooking it. Before I could decide on a plan of action, the fish moved over my hookless bait, dipped, sucked it in and swam off the same way as the mirror.

A bit dejected, I set off in search of them again but thought I had blown it. After a short while I found a group of smaller commons happily grubbing about, very close in at a depth of no more than a couple of feet. Belly crawling close to them, I was able to present a bait by casting and drawing back. The rod was gently placed in the rest with a pinch of bread as an indicator hanging at the butt. The reason for the indicator was because I could see the fish from my low level but not the bait. The fish seemed to fade away as if aware of my presence. Not wanting to waste too much time, I crawled up into a bush for a better view. My bait was visible, but the fish had gone.

Evening was drawing near, the sun was beginning to retreat like a burnt out fireball, my hopes were wearing thin. On what was by far my best ever spotting day I looked like drawing a blank. Clinging to the bush, I was daydreaming of what might have been and thinking of heading back to the van some mile and a half away. Suddenly, out of the corner of my eye, there was a dark shadow moving towards my bait. It was the big mirror again. The feeling of excitement was tremendous. I was sure that fish was going to take the bait. The whole of my body was trembling as I slid back down to my rod, and not daring to breathe, settled to await events. Almost immediately, the indicator twitched. An instant strike, and the water erupted. The situation was close to chaotic. I held on hard to prevent it from reaching a fallen tree branch some 20 yards to my right. It wasn't an especially dramatic fight, just a bit awkward due to my restricted position.

A couple of winter doubles from The Hague Canal in the mid-eighties.

An early 22lb from the Devises area that liked Robin Red.

December 1999, my first and only canal carp in the snow from Kingfisher on the way to be painted.

First carp from under The Chandlery whilst building 'Cypry'.

The roof under The Chandlery was now making fishing awkward.

First 20 from The Chandlery, a fish I caught several times.

First capture of a fish that was to become a record. Under The Chandlery at 20lb on 19th March, 2002.

21lb 4oz, 28th September, 2003.

19lb 4oz, 28th September, 2003.

The half-rotted lilies all tangled to the line, and it surged through the water like something out of Jaws. Within a few minutes a massive mirror was wallowing on the surface. I pushed the net into the vegetation, and one of the arms broke off. It must have got damaged when it was caught in the bushes earlier. There I was, the biggest carp of my life waiting to be netted and a broken net lying useless at my feet. Somehow I managed to wade in up to my knees, I laid the net beside me using one hand as a spreader block and dragged the fish over it. In one frantic move I dropped the rod, grabbed the net, lifted, and she was mine.

Lifting that magnificent mirror up the bank was the most satisfying moment of my life. I stood there soaking wet and trembling with excitement as I gazed down at it. "God, it's big!" I gasped, as I realised it must be approaching thirty. I safely secured it in a sack and set off on the couple of mile round trip back to the van to get the scales. It seemed the longest journey ever, running and panting to myself, "It must be thirty; it's got to be a thirty." Eventually I got back with the scales. The Avons hit the

An admiring glance from grandson Rhys with a winter 15lb 4oz carp that showed signs of liking Robin Red.

stop, and I knew I had more than achieved a burning ambition for a thirty. I had achieved it with a new fish and from my beloved RMC. It was later photographed and officially weighed by the club at 32lb and measured 32 inches long with a 29½ inch girth. It was a huge fish back then by any standards. It was later reported to be the biggest carp from a British canal ever, and the 8th largest in the UK that year. My fishing on the RMC for the next few years was focused on the very big common that took my hookless bait; it was big, very, very big. However, I only saw it a few more times and never had the opportunity to present a bait to it again.

In 1981 I was seconded to Nigeria by my work for about a year, which pretty much brought my marriage to the RMC to an end. The biggest lesson I had learned was to find the fish before attempting to catch them. If you think about it, a fifteen-mile stretch of canal is thirty miles of margin, that is effectively one hell of a big lake. So find them first because you can't cast to them even if they are only a short distance away. Observation, mobility, stealth and determination equals success.

After my return from Nigeria, my RMC fishing took a back seat while I concentrated on other waters. By this time carp fishing had taken off, tackle had vastly improved and bait was becoming much more available. I fished and enjoyed many varied lakes, rivers and canals in the UK, France and Holland. Caught some fantastic carp, but nothing quite came up to the mark of those early years on the RMC.

In 1985 I had a flirtation with the canals of The Hague in Holland. A fascinating place to fish, it had rows of what I can only describe as "floating cabins" on the far bank. They served as a canopy that the carp liked to get under, so of course we would always be chucking leads at the cabins, trying to get as close as possible. Yes, you've guessed it, a dodgy cast went straight through a window. That together with a constant peppering with over-shot boilies from our catapults, the residents were somewhat irate. Now an irate Dutch man, in his pyjamas, jumping and screaming from his veranda, is something to behold. He spoke better English than we did Dutch, but still could not understand the importance of getting baits under his floating cabin to catch a fish. We eventually calmed him down and paid for the window. Unfortunately, the very next day his cabin was hit again!

DETAILS OF MY DECADE ON THE ROYAL MILITARY CANAL

Year	Carp caught	Biggest	Hours fishing	Hours preparing and observing
1970	nil	nil	200	20
1971	nil	nil	220	40
1972	nil	nil	250	50
1973	5	22lb 8oz	250	100
1974	9	25lb 7oz	500	100
1975	2	8lb 9oz	280	125
1976	1	9lb 4oz	400	300
1977	1	8lb 14oz	25	150
1978	1	32lb	20	200
1979	4	26lb 3oz	70	120
1980	2	9lb	12	100
TOTALS	25	32lb	2,227	1,305

There was a hot water outlet from a factory near one area that we fished in The Hague, which resulted in some good winter fishing, even in subzero conditions when most of the other the Dutch canals were being skated on. One such time I was fishing it with fishing mate Paul Regent, the canals all around were several inches thick with ice, but due to the outlet we had plenty of clear water to fish. The downside was that every duck, coot and moorhen in Holland converged on to the area we were fishing. I remember having a screaming run resulting in a hard-fighting coot being landed, and after a few pecks and scratches removing the hook, it was released. Unbeknown to me the antics were all filmed by Paul and latterly shown, amongst other dodgy videos, on the coach trips to Cassien.

That night the temperature plummeted to something like -15c; we were absolutely bloody freezing, huddled down under only a brolly with an overwrap and wearing what was still totally inadequate winter gear. Suddenly, in the early hours, torches were shining in our face as two burly Dutch police officers muttered in broken English, "Are you alive?" Apparently, some locals who had taken an interest in the mad English camping by the canal in midwinter had called the police fearing that we had frozen to death in the exceptionally cold weather. In the midst of it all, I did manage quite a few decent fish, mostly commons up to low twenties in my time fishing The Hague canals. It was claimed by a Dutch guy we befriended that they contained many into the thirties, but we never saw anything close. However, we did, on several occasions, witness what a good set of scales he had !

In 1986 I moved with my job to Wiltshire. That move, together with a nasty divorce, buying a house with a woman who had all the symptoms of a schizophrenic psychopath, and then splitting up with her, somewhat curtailed my fishing for a while. Eventually, I got myself sorted, met and married the amazing Angie, who, singlehandedly, got me securely back on the rails.

I am now living in Chippenham, and the local canal is the Kennet and Avon. The K and A canal runs from the Thames at Reading 75 miles west to the city of Bath where it joins the Bristol Avon. It was opened as a navigable canal to carry freight in 1810 with 74 locks in those 75 miles, 28 of these on the Devises flight. In the 1950s it fell into disrepair and all but dried up until its restoration and reopening for pleasure craft in August 1990.

The K and A was a very different canal to the RMC due to it being split up into pounds between locks. Some of the pounds are an acre or two, while others stretch for about ten miles. It was in 1987, before the canal reopened, that I started to look at the possibility of fishing it for carp. Many of the pounds were very weedy and looked good prospects, as several smallish carp had been seen. I decided to bait up a pound near Foxhangers with my favourite homemade Robin Red boilies, which I was using with considerable success on a couple of local lakes. I thought it may not have been used in the area before. It was a pretty pound with lots of overhang trees on the far bank, very weedy and only about three feet deep. To heighten the enjoyment, I was to use my trusty ten-foot pound-and-a-half Richard Walkers, lovely rods that bend into the butt when playing a fish. My first few short sessions produced dozens of hard fighting fish, but only up to low teens. Size did not matter too much, as I was thoroughly enjoying the comparative peace and quiet, and I was still fishing other waters for bigger fish. I fished most of the pounds on the Devises ticket over the next few years, my favourite being the "Holiday

Cottage", named thus due to the fact it had a beautiful cottage on the north bank. It was no more than a couple of acres in size, almost totally surrounded with high reeds and rushes with a back bay behind the lock, which was thick with lilies. It had an intimacy about it that reminded me of the pretty farm ponds I used to fish as a lad. Not only did it look and feel very carpy, but it was full of carp and reputed to hold a reasonable twenty. However, one of the problems with lots of locks and pounds is that the fish do move through the locks. Sometimes this is under their own steam, but occasionally I am sure they are caught and moved by anglers trying to obscure where the better fish are. As with most of the K and A, the towpath made it difficult to set up a bivvy, and also it is a cycle way which can be a bit hazardous for anglers.

Again, although I caught a huge number of carp, none were over 19lb. What Angie, my wife did catch one afternoon though, was Patch, my lovely old dog. I was encouraging her to fish, in the selfish hope that she would get into it and want to join me more often. Anyway, there she was, doing very well catching a few on luncheon meat, but found casting a little difficult. She tended to lay the baited rig on the ground behind her and swing the rod sideways. It seemed to work ok; it just looked awkward. Patch, being a bit greedy like most dogs saw the opportunity of a free snack. Just as Ang was about to cast, after landing her umpteenth fish, quick as a flash Patch pounced on the rig and swallowed the baited hook. Ang yelled in horror and dropped the rod as the poor old dog ran hell for leather down the towpath with the rod chasing him. What a commotion! Ang and I were running down the towpath chasing the dog with him, seemingly more frightened of the rod chasing him than from the hook in his throat. It turned out ok though, and after cutting the line and taking him to the vet all Ang (well, it was her fault) had to do was feed him brown bread and sort through his poop to confirm he had passed the hook. She never did find the hook; she probably didn't look closely enough... Yuk. Anyway, he never seemed to suffer any ill effects, but the biggest tragedy was that it put Ang off fishing. However, she does still come with me on lots of my trips abroad fishing, bless her.

Up to its re-opening in 1990, Robin Red had caught me hundreds of K

A very nice linear at 16lb, July 2002.

October 2004, my first run on the new mooring. The fully scaled at 25lb.

Another pretty 14lb mirror, August 2002.

Nicely scaled mirror at 19lb 8oz, May 2003.

Returning a mint 23lb 4oz mirror, July 20th, 2003.

26lb 12oz decent mirror only seen once, January 2004.

Cyrinus was nearly finished, so I was getting out on the cut more. A pristine scrapper 20lb common, October 2005.

Fully scaled at 31lb 4oz, a new Kea PB, March 2006.

A double for grandson Harry, May 2007.

A brace of doubles with son-in-law, October 2007.

and A carp up to scraper twenties. For a few years after the opening I lost a bit of interest in it mainly due the boat traffic, but also I was doing a far bit of fishing in France with family and caravan in tow.

During the 1990s we were offered the use of a friend's 45ft narrowboat "August Folly" for a few days. We absolutely loved it and were fortunate enough to use it a few times. Our favourite mooring was by the turning bay and swing bridge at Sells Green. The canal was by then a murky brown from the disturbance of boat traffic and there was little or no weed left. But, it still fished its head off with loads of carp to mid-teens, great for the kids. Unfortunately, August Folly was sold, so that was the end of our boating, thought I.

So great was the appeal of the canal boating I knew I had to have one. By 1999 I had purchased an old dilapidated 30ft narrowboat named Kingfisher. Most of the next year was spent renovating it, we so loved that little boat. It was while taking her up to Devises for painting that I caught my first and only ever canal carp in the snow, just shy of a double, but very welcome.

It soon became apparent we needed something bigger. I sold Kingfisher and bought a 50ft sailaway hull, which I was to fit out myself, and we named her "Cypry". Now, anyone that knows narrowboats knows that the fitting out of a shell is a massive task. At the time I had a mooring under the chandlery building by the Hilperton marina. This was on a five-mile stretch of the K and A that I had not fished, and at the time I did not know if it contained carp.

The plan was to put a rod out while building the boat. This I did, most evenings, and every weekend was spent working on it, and all the time a rod would be out. Not the most attractive place I have fished, but the pod was set up in the bow so as to be clear of the low roof (chandlery floor) above the mooring, which was very awkward when netting a fish as the pontoon stopped ten feet short of the bow. I only used one rod to make it a bit less difficult. The bait was still Robin Red, and a couple of dozen baits were put in every time I was there whether fishing or not. After a few sessions I started catching bream, tench and some big eels but no carp. Not wanting to waste working time catching unwanted fish, I started making the baits much bigger and harder. Several weeks passed, and I began to think there weren't any carp in the area, but then as I was working away one evening a blistering run resulted in a 16lb common.

That fish was the first of many over the two-odd years it took me to fit Cypry out. It became almost uncanny how the bites became so regular. I would go down to the boat each evening at about 7pm, put a rod out, chuck a few baits in and then work till midnight, except for weekends, when I would stay on the boat. Ang would ring most nights at about 10.30pm, almost without exception, and if a bite was to come, it would be while Ang was on the phone. So often did this happen she had to change the time for ringing. Out of 51 carp caught while working on the boat, 29 of them came between 9.00pm and 11.00pm, and most of the rest were just before daylight. Thirteen were over 19lb, six of which were between 20lb and 22lb, a far better average than I had achieved on the K and A before. One of the 20s, caught on the 19th March 2002, was a beautiful fully scaled mirror that was to become well known to me. I in fact caught it again during the build a year later on the 3rd April 2003 at 19½lb.

Cypry was finished in 2003, and the maiden voyage was to Hungerford, because I had heard of some decent fish down that way. When we arrived there it was thrashing it down with rain, mooring was difficult, and we had to make do with a rubbish place directly outside the church. There wasn't room for the pod on the bank so it was balanced on the bow, a couple of rods quickly put out on the old faithful RR and a rapid retreat back in the boat to dry off. Ang cooked a meal, and as we sat down to eat, the remote let out a one-toner. I leapt out and pulled into what felt like a decent fish. There followed a slow, plodding fight that lasted long enough for me to get thoroughly drenched. I eventually put the net under a big mirror that weighed in at 26lb 4oz, my biggest K and A carp to date.

We spent many happy hours on Cypry, catching lots carp from all the more obscure areas of the canal that were not normally considered for fishing. We once stopped directly outside Dick's restaurant in Bradford on Avon for an evening meal. The place was heaving, and most of the dozen or more tables outside right beside the canal were taken. After the meal I decided to put a rod along the margin where lots of people were having a

22lb.

Typically nicely scaled mirror at 14lb 8oz, October 2009.

First capture of the fully scaled over the magical forty at 41lb, 29th February 2012.

28lb 4oz winter 2012.

A propeller damaged 30lb 10oz carp, May 2013.

The seventh capture of the fully scaled, what a result! A new British canal record at a massive 46lb 4oz, 15th August 2013.

A fat 28lb 4oz common, December 2013.

The latest capture of the big fully at 47lb 2oz 20th June 2014. Have I caught her too many times?

A basin caught 22lb battle scarred mirror as granddaughter Lois looks on, April 2014.

April 2014, not all the K and A fully scaled are big – a pretty 9lb gem!

A new canal PB common at 30lb 4oz.

Propeller damage healed, but down to 28lb 8oz, July 2014.

meal. My thought being, they must all throw food in for the ducks, which is affectively baiting the swim. Within an hour, off it went, producing a pristine 19lb mirror that had probably never been caught before. In fact, almost wherever we moored, I would catch a carp at some time or another.

With eight grandchildren all enjoying the boat we decided to do the build all over again but bigger, with more beds. Cypry had to be sold. We detailed the specification for the new shell and had it built to sailaway stage by Coalcraft in Rugby. When ready we took it to Stourbridge for painting and then delivered it to Hilperton in September 2005. The mooring was now a full length pontoon in the main marina basin where I was to fit her out. This time she the name chosen was "Cyprinus Carpio", ultimatly to become known as my executive bivvy.

Working on the boat in the marina was an attractive proposition from

Another fully scaled at 21lb 4oz, June 2014.

the fishing point of view, because only boat owners were allowed to fish in there. Very few of them did, so I reasoned that it would be a bit of a holding area. Also, the full pontoon made it much easier both for fishing from as well as more room for working. The format was the same as previously: I would go down to work on the boat every evening in the week then stay on at weekends. By this time I had conceded and started using readymade baits, as I was so busy. Bait was introduced and the rods put out every time before commencing work. The fit-out lasted about three years in all, and during that time I caught a lot of carp, mostly doubles with an occasional twenty-plus. Sometimes I would catch two or three in an evening, but other times I could go a couple of weeks with nothing. The vast majority were caught in the hours of daylight. With what I had experienced when under the shop out on the cut, most coming late evening and early morning, it would appear that they were patrolling out of the basin at night and back in the morning. Possibly they came in to take refuge from the ever increasing boat traffic during the day. The bream were a real problem, particularly at night, half a dozen being the norm. Bigger and harder baits helped a bit but were not a cure.

It was in the basin while doing some pre-delivery work on Cypry that I was to catch the fully scaled again. Early evening on 23rd October 2004, my first run from the new mooring resulted in landing her again weighing in at a creditable 25lb. Strangely the next time we were to meet was when Cyprinus was all but finished. I had been getting out on the cut to try her out and also do a bit of fishing, as the basin had slowed down a lot. It was 25th March 2006, I had moored up in a stretch not often fished that I had been fishing and baiting with Cotswold Tock, about three miles from the basin. A few carp had been seen in the area over the previous weeks. Two at 16lb and 23lb were caught in the night, a super result by canal standards. It was 10am, nearly time to pack up when the alarm signalled a run. As I pulled into it I knew it was a decent fish; the old 10ft RW glass rod was curved into a half circle right through to the butt as a heavy fish rolled and lunged slowly back to the waiting net. My first thought was surprise to see another big fully scaled fish from the canal. This was followed by a bigger surprise when I realised it was the same fish I had caught previously. At

Cyprinus Carpio, the executive bivvy bow exit.

Cyprinus Carpio, the executive bivvy stern exit light years from the old dug outs.

My executive bivvy, Cyprinus Carpio.

My executive bivvy, Cyprinus Carpio.

My executive bivvy, Cyprinus Carpio.

A plump mirror, 26lb 4oz.

Nice 26lb 4oz common.

A battle-scarred 23lb 8oz.

31lb 4oz, a new K and A PB, she had put on over 6lb in two years, and was more than three miles from where we last met.

Four years passed before she was to grace my net again, this time, surprisingly, back in the basin. I had not seen or heard of her being caught so had started to think she may have died or even been poached. By this time I had retired and was doing a lot more fishing out on the cut. It was a lovely sunny 21st May 2010 afternoon, very still and warm. I had long finished the boat and was down at the marina giving it a polish. The rods weren't out as I was a bit bored with fishing there, and anyway, I thought most of the carp were out of the basin doing their thing at the spawning grounds as they always do around this time of year.

There was a young couple sitting along the perimeter of the basin feeding the ducks with bread. The ducks are quite an attraction for the locals who often bring kids down to feed them. This also results in the carp having a liking for floating bread. I have had a few of them off the top, but the ducks make it next to impossible most of the time, so I don't often bother. I noticed that the couple were taking more than just a passing interest in what was taking their bread so went for a look. Sure enough, there were a number of carp fighting the ducks for the bread. How was I to resist? I went back to the boat to grab some tackle, but the trouble was, I had been sorting the gear that was kept on the boat and a lot of it was at home. I managed to cobble together an old telescopic rod with freeline crust but only had a smallish net. Regardless, I crept along the pontoon and slowly lowered the bait to what looked a decent fish, which soon drifted away. Due to the ducks, I reeled in, rebaited and waited to see another to have a go for. One of interest showed, so I dunked the crust in preparation to cast, but the fish drifted away.

Suddenly, there was a loud slurp, the rod bucked in my hand, and a fish was on. It had literally come out from under the pontoon I was standing on and taken the crust less than a yard from my feet. I'd love to say it was a dramatic fight on the old gear but it just wallowed around a bit. The biggest difficulty was getting it in the net, especially as I realised it was the big fully scaled. Somehow I managed to get it to fold into that inadequate net. When lifting it out, the realisation that it was big hit me, and a bit of panic set in, as all the gear to deal with such a fish was at home. Fortunately, I had a small mat and a sack so was able to get it quickly and safely into the sack and back in the water. As luck would have it, the chap who was feeding the ducks was a local carp angler. He kindly offered to pop and get his mat, scales and camera, which I gratefully accepted. He returned after a few minutes with all the necessary to weigh and photograph safely. She weighed in at 38lb 4oz, a new canal PB.lk I was elated, and that magnificent fish was still growing.

Over the past five years, since retiring, my fishing has intensified. I have been doing several trips to France a year, I have joined two away syndicates, and a lot of my canal fishing has been out on the cut. I still do a far bit at the mooring, but only short sessions. Also, I have fallen in love with Stuart Gillham's lake in Thailand, which I go to for a few weeks in the winter. During these last five years I have been fortunate enough to bank the big fully scaled from the K and A on three more occasions. I hope you will appreciate that I would rather not divulge the exact locations, as they are hardly fished, and I still fish them myself.

The first capture of her at over the magical forty was the 29th February 2012 at 41lb. I had been baiting steadily with 18mm Cell for several weeks and was experimenting with rock salt, which I also introduced with the Cell. The weather had improved so I decided on a two-night session. I set up late afternoon using double 18mm Cell with a third 15mm pop-up to cap it off. These were cast out with a PVA bag of rock salt and a dozen or so baits around each rod. It turned out to be one of my best K and A sessions to date. The night produced two high double commons and one lost. Just prior to first light, I had a steady take, and I was hanging on to what I knew was a big fish that fought slow and hard for what seemed ages before showing itself to be the big fully scaled again. As I lifted the net, I knew it was bigger and was not surprised when it hit the 41lb mark, another canal PB. It looked absolutely huge. I got her safely in the sack and rang my mate Charlie to do the photographs. About 15 minutes later, before he arrived, another rod shot off resulting in a mental fight and a fantastic 28lb 4oz mirror. After the ritual of photographing them both, kissing and releasing her, I settled down to a further thirty hours' blank.

Such is the canal, when they are gone, they are properly gone, maybe miles away.

August 15th 2013, after a week's cat fishing in Kent I brought my grandson, Rhys, back with me for our annual boy's fishing trip on the K and A. Our home for the week was of course Cyprinus Carpio, my executive bivvy. We were joined by my mate, Steve, to make up the team and help with the locks. The intention was to travel some distance to a more prolific carping area so that Rhys could be sure of a bit of action.

The first evening it was raining so we decided to stop early and fish an area I had been baiting for a couple of months, having seen a few good fish spawning there earlier in the year. Steve and Rhys opted to fish at the front, and I fished my baited area at the back. I baited the hairs with 15mm Cell and tipped them with 15mm cubes of homemade Cell floater cake, a method from my early days that still works well, and the bream don't seem too keen on it. Baits were cast out under the trees with 20 free offerings around each one. I had only fished the swim a couple of times that year,

A 30lb 10oz that had been hit behind the dorsal with a propeller.

blanking both times, so I was not over-confident. The plan was to move on in the morning when it should have stopped raining. At about 1.30am a one-toner resulted in a heavy but subdued fight lasting no more than five minutes. To say I was shocked to see the big fully scaled roll into the net would be a gross understatement! I could not comprehend not only the size but where she was, a place I had never expected to see her, as she would have to have gone through a few locks to get there!

We spent a few blurred minutes weighing and rechecking the 46lb 4oz weight in disbelief, a massive weight gain of five pounds in a year and a half. Pictures were taken on Steve's camera before I kissed her and gently slid her back. As I did so another screaming run resulted in a 29lb mirror. What a result! A new British canal carp record, and it was so nice that my grandson was there to see it. Strangely, just that last evening, I had been telling Steve and Rhys the stories of past captures of her and shown them pictures of her at various weights from 19lb 8oz. We moved off the next day and both Steve and Rhys had a few commons to mid-teens. I blanked, but was happy to pass the time fishing the quiver for silver fish with a big, fat smile on my face.

The latest capture was just under a year later on 20th June 2014 when she weighed a little heavier at a new British canal best of 47lb 2oz. This time I was fishing alone in an area that I had seen spawning activity and thought I saw her among them. I baited the area for a couple of weeks, this time with Hybrid. The boat was already there, as I had done a couple of blank nights earlier in the week. It was a warm, stormy feeling night and very dark. The rods were baited with double 18mm plus a 15mm pop-up to try and deter the bream. It was not until the morning that a run occurred, a short uneventful fight and there she was, that magnificent fully scaled mirror yet again. A quick phone call and my dear wife Angie came down and did the honours with the camera. Although it was a bit bigger, this capture did not give anything like the level of satisfaction that I felt the previous year. I almost felt sorry for her, and maybe I have caught her too many times and should call it a day on the K and A. However, I have since caught a new canal PB common of 30lb 4oz, a fish I have not seen before, which just goes to show, you never know for sure what's in there when it comes to canals.

I have to say that I do worry a bit about the security of canal carp. There has been a lot of poaching going on lately, particularly around the marina basin by bounty hunters sneaking in under the cover of darkness, but worst of all by eastern Europeans, laying there multi-hook lines at night. I have seen them several times, and when approached they pull in the lines and run off, most likely to somewhere else. However, since a few problems with boats getting messed with, the marina management has reported it to the police, and they do seem to be patrolling it fairly often. Of course, another danger is otters; it would be impossible to stop them if they discover the easy pickings in the canal.

There you have it: my life fishing canals. If you fancy something different to your local lakes, then check out the canals. Britain's canals are home to some very big fish, which are largely ignored by the majority of carp anglers, but, for those that are willing to put in effort to find the fish, then the rewards are there. Canal carp can be fairly easy to catch once you have found them, as they usually won't have seen much pressure. Keep a bit of bait going into an area where you have found fish and you will catch. They can be very nomadic and often only feed for short periods in any one spot. Find these hotspots and times, and then you can hone it down to short sessions. Canal carp can be spooked easily so stealth and back leads can help prevent them swimming off out of reach. Mobile floater fishing in the warmer months is very effective, but waterfowl can make it difficult.

The K and A canal contains a wide range of carp, big and small, from tatty propeller-damaged warriors through many varied and stunningly scaled mirrors, long, lean commons, classic commons and of course some magnificent full scaled gems. I have actually caught the magnificent K and A big fully scaled eight times in just over twelve years, and its incredible growth over that time can be seen in the following list of captures:

19/3/02 at 20lb; 3/5/03 at 19½lb; 23/10/04 at 25lb; 25/3/06 at 31¼lb; 21/5/10 at 38¼lb; 29/2/12 at 41lb; 16/8/13 at 46¼lb; 20/6/14 at 47lb 2oz.

The Town Stretch

By Ken South

For years I would travel past the town stretch of the canal, laughing to myself at the anglers sitting on their boxes whilst drowning maggots from their poles or float rods. How daft were they as I headed down the coast with my car loaded with my rods, brolly bait and rucksack to fish a proper carp water? I never gave the place a thought; why should I? Only nods with match rods fished it for bream and roach. Now fast forward two decades to the present, and for the last 18 months the canal has become my carp focus. Oh how things change.

The Royal Military Canal, as it is known, runs for some 27 miles along the Kent coastline from Seabrook and then cuts through the East Sussex countryside before exiting into the River Rother. This is actually the wrong way round, as it is actually this river that feeds the canal!

The canal was originally built to defend the English coastline from a possible invasion from France at the beginning of the Nineteenth Century due to a gentleman by the name of Napoleon. However, a one-armed one-eyed English gentlemen known as Nelson defeated the French fleet at the battle of Trafalgar, and the invasion never arrived. Today the French seamen seem to be preoccupied with barricading their own ports, and we now have Operation Stack! Oh how things change!

However the fact remains that the canal was built at an incredible cost to the Crown and was never ever needed to defend England. Even during the Second World War areas of the canal were identified as defensive points, and the waterway is now dotted with derelict pill boxes of various shapes and sizes. As the canal drifts out of Hythe there are even acoustic mirrors which were the predecessor to the modern radar. Even small trench systems and gun emplacements, which are now overgrown, but still visible to the trained eye, again testify to the historical military role that the canal has fulfilled throughout its 200-year-old existence.

Today some lengths of the canal have been awarded SSSI status or Site of Special Scientifc Interest. Rare flowers and fauna grow unhindered and birdlife, and wildfowl are left to their own devices. Some areas like the town stretch at Hythe are urbanised or industrialised with concrete walls, wrought iron strutted bridges and park benches, but the whole the canal is wild and wonderful. It is unique, idyllic and interesting. It is a roving angler's dream venue, which allows you a certain fishing freedom that is so often restricted on some of the better known commercial waters, and I have fallen for its mysteries, and the challenges that fishing this type of venue often throw up.

For example the carp that live in this environment are nomadic characters that do not rely on spod mix, boilies and pellets to survive and grow. They have grown to their size on a much more natural diet of bugs, berries, mussels, snails and on occasion anglers' baits such as maggots, maize and boilies when encountered.

Anglers baits will, I believe, never become a natural food source due to its 27-mile length mixed with the low numbers of anglers who actually fish the canal. This is in definitive contrast to the many modern smaller venues that have been created to feed the demands and filled with carp that have been reared on pellets and are then fed boilies on a daily basis! The canal carp travel up down the canal like wandering nomads, stopping at areas to graze on mussels, weed, snails etc. In certain areas they will often find discarded bread that has sunk to the bottom after getting past the hungry ducks and swans and seagulls.

Now being employed full time and having a family means that fishing the canal has to fit in, so almost all of my fishing takes the form of early mornings or evenings. Sometimes, when possible, I do a couple of hours during the day, but mainly I use the daytimes to walk and observe and to make notes.

My present job is shift based; one week I work evenings and finish around 2am, and this shift is followed by a week of days that commences at 10am and ends at 6pm, so typically week one, I fish early mornings after I finish my shift, 2:30am until 6-ish and then late evenings 9pm until midnight.

I have created a system to fish the canal effectively and it is one of Organised Carping Diligence or OCD. This approach sees me preparing for my session during my hour break at work, which is either my lunch or dinner break depending on the shift pattern. The chaps in the office have

The town stretch.

The first canal carp.

My first 20lb canal carp.

learnt so much about rigs, leaders and different baits over the last 18 months that I am surprised that they have not taken up carp fishing themselves! Mind you, they seem to complain about some of the smells that come from my plastic pop-up tubs, which may have a somewhat negative effect on them taking up the pursuit.

The kit I use is complete but compact. I take very little to the swim; in fact I often just carry a 3ft rod case that holds my three 9ft CQs along with my three Delks on sticks, my bait, leaders and baited rigs, landing net, headlamp, in fact everything I need to use. I then take my battered bedchair and unhooking mat. My tackle bag and other items would stay out of sight in the boot of my car.

So as I am only angling for just a few hours maximum, everything I do

The second double.

has to be quick and effective. The design of the rods I use means that they break down into three 3ft sections. Now this is great for storage and mobility, but you cannot leave them set up, so every time I fish I have to thread the line through the rods' eyes and then set up my end tackle. Now this might sound quite laborious, but in truth the way I fish this is in fact a very quick and simple operation even in the dark. I will cover this at the end, but what got me interested in the canal I hear you ask, to want fish the canal in the first place? Well I had heard rumours and mumblings about a 30lb common being caught from the canal, and this grabbed my attention as 30lb canal commons are by no means common at all, which sounds a little mixed up.

Anyway I was soon walking the town stretch on a regular basis looking for likely areas to target. My preferred method of carp fishing sees me targeting mainly marginal areas on the various waters that I have fished, as I get no enjoyment from casting to the horizon. The laying of close-in traps with simple but reliable rigs is much more me, and despite my rather large size, I love this intimate and stealth-induced style of fishing.

After much walking and investigation I settled on an area that allowed me different spots to focus on. I had discovered by casting around that one area that ran up to a bridge held an abundance of natural food in the shape of snails and very large swan mussels. In the same swim was a large willow tree with dropping branches that actually entered the water, and this area I was sure would at times hold carp. Further up the bank were a couple of mooring points, which are used in the summer months to secure the rowing boats that are available to hire. Again an area that would at certain times of the year offer the carp visiting the town stretch shelter. As far as I am aware the length of the canal that forms the town stretch had actually been flooded with concrete, so the bottom is obviously very solid, and weed growth is very isolated, and interestingly the temperature of the water is a couple of degrees warmer than the rest of the canal, a point that was going to prove to be a very knowledgeable edge in the colder months.

The clocks went back, which meant that the canal banks would become quieter, and public activity would be dramatically reduced. The first three trips passed and were totally uneventful, and I did not even hear or see any signs of fish. However I did meet an angler who informed me that no one ever fished this area of the canal, as it never produced any carp! This was just what I wanted to hear after my hard work through the summer. With his departure I sat there basically sulking and wondering how I could have got it so wrong. But then, and totally out of the blue, the green LED lit up as the right hand rod pulled round. A take! I could not believe it. I picked the rod up and I was attached to my first ever canal carp. The fight was frantic, as the fish ran up and down in front of me. Maybe I was nervous and did not want to risk losing the carp, but the fight seemed to go on and on. Actually it probably did not last that long, and I pulled the grey fish over the net cord. My first canal carp was mine, and I quickly set up my cradle and got my camera ready.

Whilst I was sorting all this out a car pulled up behind my swim. A chap

The 20lb common.

got out and said "Have you got one?" "Yes," I said as he made his way down the bank. Now I noticed that he was looking a bit wet, which struck me as strange as it had not been raining. The guy turned out to be an angler by the name of Ian, and he had been fishing below a bridge further down when a rather drunk person walking across the bridge decided to have a wee. How unlucky was that. Anyway due to being pissed on Ian decided to pack up. I got the carp out of the net and Ian kindly took some pictures of a very grey looking fish. Ian left after congratulating me, and I wiped my camera with a Dettol wipe!

Over the winter I struck to my plan and continued to fish either dark, early, cold and damp mornings or late, dark, cold and damp evenings! Somehow they all seemed the same. The winter weeks passed, and I was very fortunate that I managed to catch a couple of upper doubles in the shape of a mirror and an immaculate common. I also caught a lovely near-leather of 25lbs just before the traditional Christmas lay-off as family.

The New Year arrived, and so did the carp shows. Following the Brentwood Show I was in attendance at The Big One. As usual I returned

The 30!

home late on the Sunday night to a sleeping family. Monday was spent sorting my tackle box out, as it always gets in a real mess following the weekend rig demos. I awoke early and I decided to brave the cold, damp, and now wind and set off down to the swim.

Amazingly after a couple of hours I had a take from under the willow, and after a very nervy fight where the carp took me very close to some sunken branches I managed to land my first 20lb canal common carp. I was totally made up, and as I snuggled back down in my sleeping bag the heavens opened and the rain fell. Boy, did it fall. I pulled the sleeping bag up over my head, but the rain just continued, and soon I was soaking and feeling rather cold. I wondered why I was still there suffering when the same rod cast back to the same place pulled round, and the alarm let out its high pitched squeal. Soaking and cold I lifted the rod and struck into the fish. The carp kept to the bottom, and my blue-coloured hands felt quite numb, as the rod was wrenched to the left and the right. Eventually I decided that enough was enough, and I just held the rod up high and leaned back, making sure that I didn't slide on the sea of mud that had appeared. I took my other landing net and threw it in the water as I pulled the carp up. The fish went into the submerged net first time, and I bit the line and chucked the cold, wet carbon stick up the bank.

I then secured the landing net complete with carp to the bank with a brolly peg. After unhooking the carp in the net, I jumped backed into the now saturated sleeping bag due to it being left open whilst I played and landed the fish. As I pulled the cover over me I wondered if I was actually wetter than the two carp that were now retained awaiting the arrival of Ian to take the pictures. I lay there soaked and cold and wondered why I had brought a couple of brolly pegs but left the bloody brolly at home.

Bang on time Ian arrived fully suited, as he works in the City. As he changed his shiny shoes for his muddy wellies I got the camera ready and lifted the first carp into the cradle. Ian took the pictures and said what a great result catching a twenty-pound canal common was for such a horrible night, especially as it was February. As if I needed reminding as I knelt there freezing, soaking, and as I moved, squelching.

I returned the common to its watery home and started to lift the second net out of the water. Ian sad, "You never told me you had caught another!" "Oh, I'm sorry… I must have forgotten in all that freezing rain… please forgive me," I replied, as I started to lift the net. Ian started to gasp and point as the fish came up through the depths. I looked down and actually saw the fish for the first time, as I'd landed it in the dark because my head torch was covered in mud. The carp was a proper big'un and a common at that. Ian suggested that this could be the thirty, the only 30lb common in the seven-mile stretch. All of a sudden I could understand why he had that job in the City after all. As I placed the common into the cradle I felt myself laughing. I don't know if this was because I had not even realised what I had caught in the early hours on a cold, wet, dark morning in February or because I had caught, as Ian said, the only 30lb common in the canal.

Suddenly I wasn't feeling cold or even wet! Oh how things change!

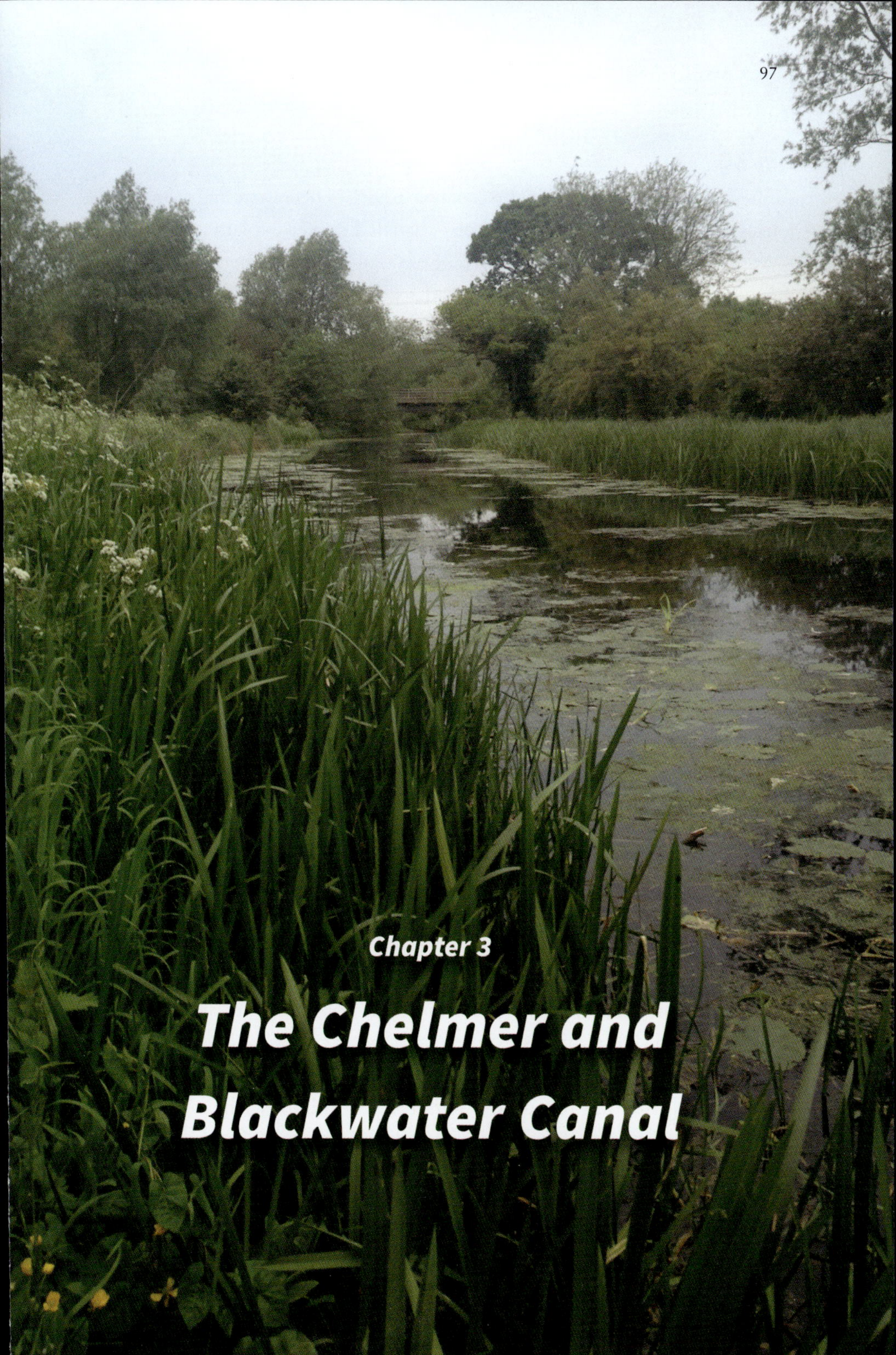

Chapter 3

The Chelmer and Blackwater Canal

Mystery and Secrets

By Matt Lee

The mystery and secrets of the canal have always been niggling at me in the back of my mind for more reasons than I can ever explain. It all started years ago when I was a curious young lad that needed something to occupy me in my spare time and school holidays and to keep me out of trouble. I asked in the local tackle shop what was the cheapest and easiest way of catching a fish from the canal. Off I wandered to the canal with my new sparkly spinner in the hope of catching a prickly perch.

After a long, hot wait getting sweaty and irritated I was about to give up when I flicked my spinner out for the last time, only this time I was fishing alongside a stationary boat. Within seconds the rod tip bounced and I had my first perch. After catching a few of the stripeys I noticed a dark shadow move out from under the boat, and my curiosity was sparked. After watching the shadow for a few minutes I realised it was a carp. I followed the shadow with baited breath until I reached a floating pontoon, where to my amazement sat 15 carp basking in the sun, six of the carp being the size of my arm! My adrenaline was pumping through body; I needed to catch one of those beasts.

I remembered passing a man along the canal path who was match fishing, so I went back to him as quickly as my feet could take me. When I got to him I explained my excitement at what I had seen further down the bank, he looked at me and smirked, then told me that I wouldn't catch them on the tackle I was using. After some deliberation the man reluctantly gave me a size 12 hook and six slices of bread, but he was adamant that a lad of my age would never catch a canal warrior. With my new tackle and bread in hand I was full of determination to prove the man wrong. I scurried back to the pontoon in the hope that the carp would still be basking in the summer sun.

When I returned to the pontoon they were all still basking. I wasted no time and flicked my bread out. Within a few minutes I heard a massive slurp and I was hooked into my first dark canal warrior. The fight was like nothing I had experienced before. After landing my second carp the lock keeper was on my back, giving me grief about no fishing near the boats. I moved off, unhappy and disheartened, but I wasn't going to give up that easily; I wanted the big mamma I had seen earlier. I waited 30 minutes before returning to the basking spot. I caught a further two carp and I lost one that can only be described as Jaws. I was then thrown off again by the grumpy lock keeper. I took his advice this time but this would be the turning point of my carp adventures.

Over the next ten years I built up my carp fishing gear and joined various associations, clubs and many day ticket waters. I even ventured to France a couple of times but nothing matched the exhilaration, adrenaline or excitement that the canal gave me. I gave into the temptation of the canal and started the hunt for my childhood mystery all over again, only this time I had a bit more knowledge of carp fishing, but I also had to fish whenever I could due to acquiring a wife and two beautiful daughters.

I spent every hour I could rowing up and down the canal with a couple of mates on the lookout for signs of the mysterious carp. We found numerous signs and locations of the big warriors, and this is where the passion was reignited. I would return to the locations that we had found armed with buckets of particle, pellets and boilies on the hope of enticing my mystery secrets to feed and be confident.

Over the time I landed a few carp but nothing to shout about, but I knew the big girls where still out there. I tried fishing over snags, lilies, in the tight margin and open water using a basic blow back rig with double bottom baits, coating my gripper leads with paste and filling the middle with oil attractant so when the paste breaks down the oil sweeps along the water and attracts the curious carp with bursts of flavour. I tried to keep everything simple, as most of the carp have never experienced rigs or never been caught. I caught numerous single and mid double carp using this technique but still hadn't tricked the bigger, wiser carp.

I observed the canal for many years where the boats were moored and realising this is where my childhood secrets and mysteries were hiding. The only problem I came across was there is strictly no fishing where the big girls were. I used to find every excuse to walk the canal, even taking the wife and the girls for a day out to watch the canal for carp. The girls fed the ducks, and the wife thought I was taking her to the pub for lunch, but

Standing at the mouth of the lock before it enters the sea – pukka.

Lovely sunrise as I'm leaving the canal, which I normally miss.

Caught at the tips of my rods in thick lilies... Sshhhh!

Same session – thick lilies hook and hold... Sshhhh!

Unique torpedo-shaped carp fight the best.

This common really gave me a challenge; I had to jump over boats to land it.

The unique SS4 range doing it for me... Sshhhh!!

Simple blowback rig nailed most of my fish. (Right) Secret squirrel – staying stealthy and keeping out of sight is a challenge on its own.

actually I was still chasing my dreams, and everyone was happy. Once the family are tucked up for the night that is my opportunity to creep along the towpath in search of my dream fish.

I tucked myself and all my gear up beside a crane or a dry docked boat so I was virtually invisible, setting my rods up in the pitch dark with only the moonlight to guide me. I put Blue Tac over my Delkim lights, and the tone on minimum so it was almost inaudible to the human ear. I put my traps in place using an old 13 metre match pole to push my lead under the boats for perfect positioning, and it was a sit and wait process, making sure I was out of sight, using the crane as a bed chair, and my unhooking mat and bag for a bit of comfort.

I had just got into position and set my rod beside the boat, I had taken the protective tip off of my second rod and I had a screaming one-toner. The rod had bent over and the butt end came off its resting place. I ran to the rod and struck into a dead heavy weight. I set my clutch tight and applied pressure. All it felt like was a dead weight holding the bottom and stripping line into open water. It started kiting right towards the row of stationary boats, which were three deep.

I knew I was in severe danger of losing it, so I lowered my rod tip into the water and nearly buried the tip into the silt, keeping my line as close as I possibly could to the bottom, hoping that I could deter the fish from heading towards the boats' propellers. I tried holding pressure and to gain line on the fish, but when most of the rod is in the water it's impossible to know where the fish is. I lifted the rod a little just to see where the fish was, as I had already managed to gain a lot of line back. My heart was pounding and my legs shaking as the fish was now at the bow of the boat. I knew now that I could start to fight the fish properly and it was now in my control. My rod was still doubled over with the carp just under my rod tip in the deep margin hugging the bottom. I knew this was going to be a very big mystery warrior.

I had never had a carp hold the bottom like this before, and my adrenaline was racing. The carp decided to take a powerful lunge forward into open water, but my clutch was set tight so it made the carp rise through the layers of water. I had so much pressure on it that it made the

A solid common – hard work really paying off.

Sleeping on a crane and staying light, stealthy and out of sight.

(Left) Keeping it real – most of my fishing is done under the stars.
(Below) Myths mysteries and achievements are made from effort and hard work.

beast come up and take a huge gulp of air. I knew I had to try my best to hold it there. I managed to slip the net straight under the warrior, and it went head first into my net. I was delighted, and I punched the air with a silent shout. I couldn't believe my eyes when I looked down into my net at my achievement – all my hard work was starting to pay off. I was chuffed, as it was a great result for only having my rod in the water for five minutes.

Where I fish there is a working lock nearby the last lock, which goes out to sea, and with the lock gates in constant use the carp and bream are attracted to the influx of salt water, which helps them clean and flush their gills. I always keep a tide table in my bag so I know in advance when the salt content is at its highest. As a family man my sessions are very limited and are usually only five hours long, normally midnight until 5am. I'm always packed up and at work whatever the weather. I have caught a few 20lb-plus carp; they fight unbelievable hard, fast and strong – a lot like torpedos. Most of my captures I like to keep secret, like the canal mysteries!

I have been lucky and honoured enough to be a team member of pukka Squirrel Baits. With the Smurf 'the traveller' Marc Twaite's brains and knowledge behind them gives me confidence, and it's the only bait range I'm aware of that's got 100% natural ingredients in both the ranges that are highly soluble and digestible fishmeals. The SS4 and GS4 ranges have transformed my angling, singling out the bigger carp. I try to prebait and keep my spot primed as much as I can, and without fail the night before I go I give them a good few kilos of boilies.

The mystery continues… I know there are uncaught canal carp with no name, and I will continue to work hard, keep the bait going in, keep the family happy and enjoy every moment on the bank chasing dreams.

Until next time… Sshhhh!

Follow my adventures on twitter: matlee198787.

Canal Life

By Jade Martin

With the canal being no more than a five-minute car journey from my home in Maldon, Essex, it was near impossible not to glance at it and want to have a wander. The canal has turned up fish to 34lb-plus including mirrors and commons as well as large perch – maybe to me one day!

Persuading Dad to even teach me to fish had been hard enough, and having only been fishing a few weeks we decided to start prebaiting for the opening night on the canal. We made it our thing and used it as a very good excuse to use the wasted evenings after dinner we would have spent lounging!

We began baiting three spots, one of which was clear and which we monitored each time we visited. The others we planned to fish, one off the bank edge and the other in the river flow. The walks included bridges and locks, which we would climb up to look over and hope to catch a glimpse of a carp scouting through, which we did see on quite a few occasions just next to the local Tesco! One of them was what we believe to be a dark 25lb-plus common.

The first night we fished we gulped our dinner down, packed the last bits up and went to the canal. We took minimal gear and carried it from the car to our spot. We set up by the side of the canal, needing to leave spaces for dog walkers and 4am runners, which was pretty much impossible. We found our beds invaded by weeds, and of course crawling with spiders, which meant I was wrapped up in my sleeping bag without any air seeping in all night. Rods out and brollies up, we sat together on my Dad's bed just taking it all in. Not ten minutes later our faces were lit up by my alarm's white LED. We both just looked at each other and waited at least ten seconds before launching onto my little dwarf rod.

This fish had come from the gap between the two trees, and I was just hoping I would get to see it. 30 seconds into the fight I thought I'd lost it; it was bringing in a ton of weed, and I just didn't feel any connection. Dad took my rod and got the fish kicking again, but we were both still in shock, and we were hardly saying a word! Dad leant down and netted the weed bed for me, or it may as well have been, as I still hadn't seen anything but

a tail swish at this point.

Before even unhooking the fish he grabbed me in a massive bear hug, and we jumped up and down like kids at Christmas. People walking dogs (at 10pm at night) would seriously question our sanity. With the high-fiving over we were ready to see what creature we had caught! Slowly picking away at the weed we unhooked the fish, my little pink pop-up and chod perfectly intact amongst tangles. While I got my waders on and prepared the mat I just saw an enormous grin light up my dad's face. This was a PB for me at the time – a great achievement for us after months of preparing. Laying the fish on the mat after weighing it at 17lb 7oz, we looked at it, motionless, as if it was working us out. It probably had not been caught before, and if it had, it hadn't been for a while. Its mouth was perfect, and its body covered in little scars and marks as well as being a colour I'd not seen on a carp before.

I sat down ready for photos. The fish had a completely different aura to the other fish I'd caught, showing perfect behaviour. We had a few bank photos, and then I got into my waders for my first ever water shot. I slid down the bank into the water without a care for how cold the water was rising up my arms! After a few more photos with a massive grin on my face, I let it go back into the canal. It swam off quickly, spun round, and just sat in the weed not a metre from my foot. I got out, keeping an eye on him, but he soon swam off. It was an amazing feeling.

Following that I then topped that week with two more PBs from a local day ticket, first a 22lb common and then a 26lb 8oz mirror. To this day, even after having fish to 52lb in France, my favourite and most memorable will be that canal fish. Unfortunately that night was the last night for Dad and me due to the shop getting incredibly busy, until a couple of weeks after when I sprung it on Dad that we should go down there for the evening, and so we did… With the rods out and sat back again on our chairs my rod went off again. It honestly felt like nothing was on there, but I brought in this little baby 2 or 3lb mirror. We decided to stay even though it started raining. We braved it for a while until our seats started to collect water and then called it a day. We walked back into our house drenched, and all for a baby fish!

We continued to bait until the season closed, as then the paths become very overgrown and it's pitch black before we get home. We began prebaiting again this year and spent a short evening fishing just two rods between us, which resulted in nothing, although we know it won't be long!

A Whole New World!

By Matt Lee - Pukka Squirrel Baits

Canal carp are something special; they are unique. With time not on my side this season to do any kind of campaign, I have had to drop in on the odd free night I have had spare In between family and work commitments in the hope that my watercraft knowledge from the results from sessions in the past could pick me out the odd carp in quick overnight session. 2014 the opening night of the 16th saw me have one of my best nights to date with seven carp over the space of five hours with one of the mirrors being my darkest, best looking carp I have had from the canal down south where I live in Essex. It was a torpedo-shaped black mirror that almost ripped the rod from my hands during the battle. The same night saw me have my first zip linear, which in a few years will put a few smiles on a few faces that ever wish to give the canal a go. The season soon flew by, and I only managed the odd night every two weeks. Nothing special had graced my net other than many small commons throughout winter.

With the season over for a few months it was time to rethink an approach for the upcoming season. With a plan ready and for a change not working alone, we decided on a certain boat, and at both ends baited hard with a boilie-only approach of chops, whole and crumb. I had gone with the awesome Sweet Candy SCS4 from Pukka Squirrel Baits. The reason for this was that water levels in canals and rivers can differ from floods, and being a high attract instant bird food boilie it's pukka for a silty, murky bottom. I was armed with double hard hookers on one rod on a simple blowback rig incorporating the C430 hooks from Ashima, which I have great confidence using in snags and around the boats and barges. I used a Sweet Candy SCS4 14mm pop-up on a stiff hinge rig on my other rod, using an indispensable C410 hook. Both the rigs and hooks that have done me well over the last few seasons on these hard-fighting carp.

The swim.

Stunning dark scaly canal mirror, they don't come any better. Sweet Candy doing it!

Mint zip linear, what a stunner.

Another angry dark wild mirror from the canal.

Black canal mirror, just how we like 'em.

Just before getting caught on the boats at 7am.

Pukka Squirrel Baits SCS4, 100 per cent confidence, love it!

'Keeping It Real' team, PSB style.

Sshhhh!!

June the 15th came round, and we were sat on the footpaths ready to be casting in at midnight. It was a quiet night for me, but my friend opened his account up with an upper twenty shortly after midnight. After that all went quiet, and the only alarm I heard was for getting me up for work. Half an hour after leaving I had a phone call telling me that it had all kicked off with my friend having a double take. Before he left he had four carp. I was buzzing for him that the spots were producing so soon. We were both buzzing that the Sweet Candy was doing its job instantly. With the bait going in regularly the spots were throwing up carp on most sessions. A month or so passed, and the platforms we were fishing from became home to a few resident boat owners, so the fishing came to another halt for me. I tried moving their mooring ropes and tying them off at different points so I could get the rods in and land fish safely, and then replacing them as I left for work. After a few weeks people started living on the boats so that put a stop to me straight away, and it was more effort gone out the window, as it was not safe for me to stay.

It was very frustrating, and there were rumors going about that there was a new lock keeper who was cracking down on the strictly no fishing from the pontoons and between the boats. After hearing a few people getting caught and arrested I let it be for a while before having another go. On my return our spots were still a no-go, so I was just dropping in on free platforms and casting in as and where I could with no prebaiting, just turning up and putting a few kilos of Candy chops and pellet out, hoping to stop any passing carp. Using this approach on just five-hour sessions was hard going, but every other session I was getting bites, so I was happy even though I could get caught at any time. It was a real buzz chasing canal carp under those circumstances. Every bite is a result for me, and size doesn't even come into it, but when they do come along you definitely know about it; they are wild and really scrap till the end.

The start of September I had a screaming take where both rods were going nuts. Waking up in a daze, I struck the wrong rod then left it slack as I struck the right rod. It was an epic battle with a very angry mirror that just would not come in without a fight. I realised the carp had picked up my other line, and trying to net it became hard, as it was dragging a 5oz lead and line through the thick cabbages just under the surface. She finally gave in, and I was looking her at the bottom of my net. I was made up, staring at one of the best looking mirrors I've had to date. With daylight due within the hour, I left her to recover and to get a better look at her for some pictures.

Since then I have done just two quick nights that have resulted in a lovely dark common to start my autumn campaign. Again the Sweet Candy has been doing me proud. I know I'm going to be watched, and I know it's going to be very hard work, but I also know the rewards are there. I'd much rather catch the unknown from a tricky canal than fish any kind of commercial overstocked fishery all day long. One stunning wild carp from the canal is worth ten Simmo stocked carp from day ticket waters, plus I get a real buzz from the chase, not just with carp but the boat owners and bailiffs. That's what it's all about for me and the team at Pukka Squirrel Baits, keeping it real. Watch this space! There's more to come...

Chapter 4

Canal Catches

Canal Carping UK

By Nick Mays

These are just a few of the fish if had in four years on the GUC and Oxford canal around Rugby. From the first canal carp to the biggest at 26lb 2oz we made Canal Carping UK about four years ago, and it's good too see carp from all over the UK. I've got a lot of pics, but these are some of my most memorable catches.

Canal Carping UK was originally started by my friend Chris Thomas around five years ago; we were just a few lads with the same passion for catching carp. One of the people we worked with mentioned a local marina that he knew had good fish in, as he fed them off his boat.

Not being a fisherman, he just said that some of them must be nearly three feet long, so we all thought they sounded like fish worth having a go at. I think a massive part of fishing the canal is the unknown. So we started putting some regular session in on that stretch; blanks became the norm,

and it was a carper's nightmare with bream after bream, but we believed that there were carp in the area.

After a change of our spot, we finally got amongst the carp, which were pound for pound a much better stamp of fish compared to lakes, and it wasn't costing us tickets as no club ran the stretch we were fishing. I soon fished the canal full time up to three nights a week and was given other local areas to try by boaters. Before we knew it, it was hard to choose where to fish.

Some spots could do a couple of fish but others better fish. In my four years of canal carping I'd done a number of 20s to 26 with only a handful under 10lb. I had plenty of blanks and bream between but that's all part of canal carping.

So the page was mainly to share knowledge and experiences with each other across the UK about what is working rig and baiting wise. It's far from easy going on the canal, but with our page you can get useful tips from many experienced canal carpers up and down the country who are fishing them on a regular basis. Not many will tell you exact spots but will point you in the right direction. I think finding those nomadic carp is a big part of the fun because it's the largest water you can fish in UK, and it can be hard going.

'The One'

Aaron Isherwood

I first saw this fish on the Northern Carp Anglers' Facebook page and was simply amazed at the photo. The caption was 31lb 11oz. I didn't hesitate to send the captor a message, but fair play to him; he chose to keep it under wraps, and I'm glad he did. After a little digging around I started to suspect where the fish resided; it was a water I had already started fishing and the fish were all unknown – nobody bothered with then much at all. I had always known there were carp in there but every capture would be a surprise – just how I like it. The venue is an off the beaten track section of a northwest canal. I had started wandering it more and more when I recognised a section of guttering on a house in the background that

matched the house on the photo from Facebook. That will do me, I thought, and I was off.

The water became my main target water, and I enjoyed some real close encounter stalking and a little "guesting" at night, which was completely against all rules but that's how it got me; it was right under my skin. I had eight different fish up to 26lb 2oz before I finally became aquatinted with "The One". All these fish were stunning dark, scaly mirrors, and I'm so privileged to have caught them. It was 12 months after starting my campaign when I got down on a cold, foggy late October morning. I had found the fish in the usual area, and I managed to get a rod in position 3ft from the bank without any disturbance. A handful of hemp with a white Northern Special fished Withy Pool style was the downfall of this incredible creature.

I watched it come in and feed, and then it just went mental and shook its head violently from side to side before bolting out of the swim leaving

my clutch spinning. After a short, hairy battle victory was mine and the fish was in the net. Adrenaline took over and the rest is a blur. After a quick call to my good friend Si, he was on his way with the camera and to help out with weighing. For the record the fish was 28lb 12oz but that really didn't matter – I was overwhelmed with what had just happened and couldn't stop staring at the photos for weeks after. These fish mean a lot to me now, and I was in two minds whether to publish this or not, but I think fish like this just have to be shared. I hunted it, I found it, I baited and I caught! Get out and look for them – you never know what you might find.

North West Canal Carping

By Liam Webster

After getting bored of my usual spots and getting a lot of repeat captures, I was thinking of a new challenge after. I'll come back to that spot shortly and its carp, one of them being what I think is the largest resident of that length of murky canal, The Pet I call it. I first caught this fish around 2006 at a nice chunky 25-plus, and over the years it's fallen to various tactics from floating baits to boilies and meat. At a rough calculation, I've had this fish once or twice a year since the first capture, and the biggest it's topped my scales is 26lb 15oz.

So the big move... I arrived at my new destination not knowing what was in there. I started off by baiting it quite heavily with lots of pellet and boilie. The first few sessions were rather slow without seeing a fish and not a bleep apart from one early morning run around 6am, which ended up escaping by cutting me off, sadly. A day or two passed again, and this time a tea time bite and bang! The same thing again! Gutted! Two got away, so time for a change. I robbed some GR60 off my mate in 15lb, loaded up with that, and then 20ft of Amnesia and 10ft of leadcore. I got the rods back on the spot. Another day passed with me thinking I'd done my chances when out of nowhere there was a big eruption and bang! It was out the clip and it was fish on! After a hectic five-minute battle this beautiful creature graced my net. Was I happy? Only 24lbs, but what a stunning fish! I fished the spot quite heavily for another two weeks and had three other

fish, but none of any decent size.

A few months later, one early morning I was back to my new area, and a change of tactic with some early morning surface fishing. It's my favourite time to fish canals, as it's nice and peaceful and boat free (big smile). I put out a few pouches of floaters and relaxed. I'd set up, easy and simple as you get, with 8lb line straight through to a size 6 wide gape. Literally as I was tying my hook on, all I heard was a big slurp, and looking around wondering whereabouts it came from, I saw a back stick out the water. A head rose and took another, then slipped down. While frantically putting some bread on the inevitable happened, and it disappeared.

I waited ten minutes, and it was back, behaving the same again, taking a few and then disappearing. I flicked my bread out to the area, and in a flash it took it. I waited to see my line move so I knew it definitely had it properly in its mouth. It feels like a lifetime, but it all happens in a second. So, within a second it had me under a boat, so I dipped the rod underwater, slowly started to retrieve the fish from under the boat. Within a few tense

minutes the battle was over with this nice mid-20 that could be one the ones that cut me off earlier in the year; we will never know.

After arriving at the canal midday with the sun shining brightly, I knew the fishing wouldn't be easy, so armed with just rod net, floaters, scales and mat, I went on my way. On days like this the fish are usually easy to find, cruising up and down and just chilling in the shallower water in the edges. The first half hour passed by, but I saw nothing but boats and plenty of them, which was probably the reason the fish were on the quiet. I carried on walking and ended up going a lot further along the canal than usual, about two or three miles down the length where I knew there was a large reedbed. Arriving there I headed to the middle of the reeds, which are all along the far bank, probably 300 yards of them, with a bit of a hole in the

James Willets with a lovely dark common at 12lb 9oz.

middle. I got a few handfuls of floaters and threw them tight against the reeds and into the gap in them, the mixers needing to be tight to them so when the boats pass by some of your bait stays where you want it instead of getting washed away with the tow.

Looking over, I noticed a swirl and a fish took a mixer then another. Then a boat came and the fish dropped down and disappeared. This happened over and over again, probably three or four times the boats just kept coming until I noticed the water go completely still. This is normally good sign, and there are no boats for ten minutes or so. That was my chance, so I put a quick handful of mixers in the gap and the bait was flicked over, just hanging off the reeds nicely so on the take it would just pull off, but wouldn't move with a tiny bit of tow. A few later the fish was

James Willets with a common at 10lb 1oz.

back slurping away when its head turned and bang! It took the hookbait, and after quite a short fight this old character slipped over the net cord. I felt like giving up many times that day, but I'm glad I didn't!

Grantham Lincolnshire Canal

By James Willets

These are a few of the canal carp I have caught this year on my local stretch of canal. I've fished the stretch since I was a kid, as it's literally a stone's throw from the house I grew up in, and I'm still fishing it to this day.

There aren't a lot on this stretch, just a small family, but they can be very tricky to catch with the pressure of the public fishing it too.

James Willets with a lovely little dark mirror of 9lb 10oz.

A lovely mirror, which is the biggest I've had this year off the canal at 17lb 9oz.

I've been on and off the canal all year, as there are a few carp on the stretch I am targeting at the moment that I feel will pay off before winter.

I keep all my rigs simple and found prebaiting at night works well.

All the fish were caught on the same rigs. I fish the canal all year round in my home town of Grantham, Lincolnshire leading up to Nottingham.

Opening Night

By Luke 'Sparky' Sparkes

Well, my opening night on the canal could not have gone any better. I had a couple of snotties aka bream through the night, and at 3.30am this morning my left rod purred off, wiping my other rod out in the process. After one or two hairy moments throughout the fight, in the end I won the battle. It was my first carp on the bank and a personal best for the canal, a lovely common of 16lb 4oz.

Luke Sparkes with a lovely common at 16lb 4oz.

Various Contributors' Catch Reports

Aaron Isby – a northern disused canal.

Ben Leuty.

Jay Hampsted with a lovely old canal character of 21lb 8oz.

James Little, 17lb 7oz, Grand Union.

Jimmy Griffin, canal in the Marne Valley, France, 44lb 1oz.

John Ball.

John Ball.

John Ball.

John Ball.

Mark Harrison, 25lb 10oz on the Viking Baits' brown tigers, half an hour after chucking the sticks out.

Simon Taylor, Bude Canal, Cornwall. Not as big as the rest of the country down here, but still pretty though.

Ben Leuty.

Basingstoke Canal – Kieran Lewis caught this 35lb canal mirror (nickname Cracker) on a Sticky Baits 16mm Krill boilie with a 12mm Buchu Berry. he fished to a clear spot 50 yards away with 1kg of the Krill 12mm boilies baited tightly. It's truly a stunning fish and a new personal best! He also had three more fish at 10lb, 15lb and 16lb, and was only fishing for roughly four hours! It was definitely the best session of his life and will take a lot to beat!.

Nick Allen with a nice common at 21lb.

Grand Union Canal, Dean Keenan – I caught it out of the Grand Union Canal at Northolt, weighing 21lb this summer. It's a personal best mirror from the canal so far, and I was using Tutti Frutti boilies.

Cheshire Canal – Adam Arathoon from Ellesmere Port, Cheshire caught this 23lb 4oz mirror from a local canal. He had been baiting the spot for a while and had a few double figure fish from this area, including some lovely commons. This was his sixth fish and the biggest so far. He caught the fish in 3ft of water on a light area of silt with a scattering of boilies over the top.

Basingstoke Canal

When Marco White first turned up to my swim at the Basingstoke Canal, it was a good 20 degrees Celsius and the wind was blowing a gale and some! He had a little feel around with a 1oz lead and found a very nice hard spot at roughly 10-11ft deep. He put a rig out nice and early to see if he could get an early bite, but all he got was a crayfish nightmare and had no choice but to reel in and rethink rigs. He left it till early evening before placing a rig in again, and by that time the crayfish weren't a problem.

It got to midnight and to his surprise, still no bites. The rigs were perfect; the weather was right but not a touch. He waited up until 3am and still nothing. He knew something wasn't right, so reeled in, slightly tweaked his rigs and a few handfuls of bait later, the rigs were back out. By 5:30am he was shocked that he hadn't had a bite yet, so he had to make a recast, but only on one rod. And it was that recast that made all the difference, and it resulted in an absolute cracker of a fish – a 20lb 6oz single scaled mirror that put up one hell of a fight! He asked around the local carping anglers and the bailiffs and they had never seen that fish before, so that made him even happier. It just goes to show that a few tweaks and recast can make all the difference.

Staffs Canal

By Tony Powell

I got to do a few sessions on the Staffs canal this summer and caught this one just before dark, which is unusual for this stretch of the canal. It weighed 30lb 4oz and was one of three thirties I have caught out of the cut this year. It's actually the smallest of the three, but unfortunately I did not get any pictures of the others as no one was around.

The 29lb from the same spot.

Not the best photo but definitely my best canal capture, a 25lb 8oz koi, Ry Don.

James Little, 25lb on the nose, Grand Union.

The Sankey Canal

By Les Stewart

The black mirror weighed in at 16lb 7oz, probably my favourite carp I've caught. The first common was 11lb 4oz, the second mirror was 10lb 8oz and the second common was 7lb 5oz, all caught from various sections of the Sankey Canal.

MARK

PALLATRAX

Trent and Mersey Canal

By Stuart Hydes

This 33lb 4oz two-tone mirror was caught from the Trent and Mersey canal back in May 2015. I caught it on a four-hour session only taking one rod, fishing a solid bag of crushed boilie and micro pellets with a snowman style setup, 18mm bottom bait and a pink pop-up, both Mainline Cell.

Grand Union Canal, Milton Keynes

By Michael Humphrey

28lb-plus.

20lb-plus.

26lb-plus.

27lb.

26lb.

22lb.

Worcester Canal

By Jake Harvey

I've been baiting a spot on the canal for a long period of time but couldn't get time for a session. I was baiting with Nash TG Active and managed five and lost three using Key Cultured hookbaits. I was fishing them on a blowback rig with a size 6 shot just under the bait (I'm a Nash fieldtester, hence why I'm using all the products). I basically ended up with five up to the 22lb koi, but have had over 20 fish over the course of the year.

Walsall Canal

By Richard Ball

A few that I have managed to get this year so far from a few spots around Walsall. There are a few 30s in there.

Grand Union Canal Session

By Tim Barrett

Here is a mid 20, a lower 20 and a double, all minters taken from same spot on the my first proper canal session from the Grand Union Canal.

SATROCK

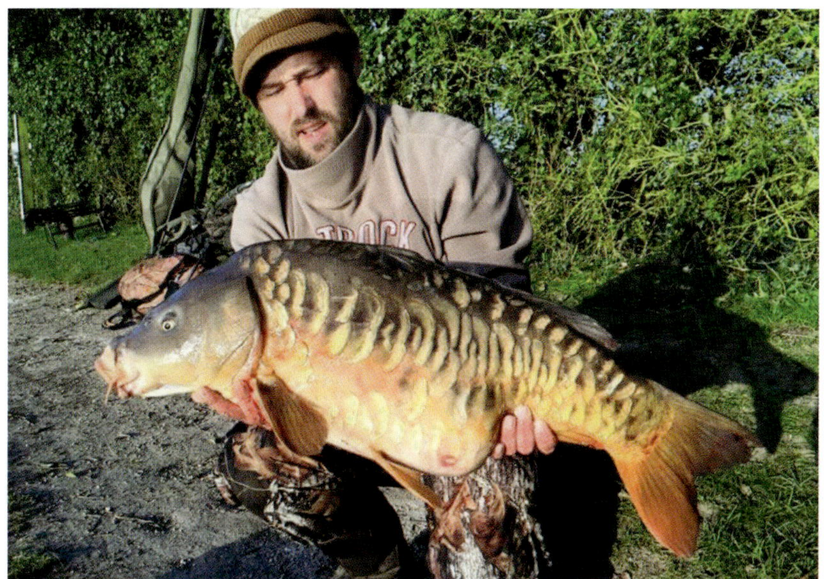

My Target Fish

By Craig Evans

It was after a big discussion with my mate that we decided to fish a part of the canal that's known for being weedy. After finding a peg that was fishable, we got the rods out. I'd chosen to fish a V-shape, clearing on the edge of a big patch of weed. I decided to bait it with a mix of hemp, boilies and maize from Beechwood Baits. My weapon of choice on the hook was a pure white Musselberry hi-attract pop-up fished on a chod tight to the weed. With rods locked tight we retreated to the warmth of our bags. We had nodded of without knowing, because at 2am I was awoken by a few single bleeps. Staring hard at my rod through the misty fog I could see the bend was not normal, so I hurried out my bag and picked up the rod to feel a big lump on the end, which decided it would dart uncontrollably to the reeds where it locked me up. After half an hour of leaving the line slack, I was just about to give up when click, click, click, and it was taking line. I hit hard into the fish, and to my amazement it slipped out of the reeds. After another 30 minutes of scrapping she rolled into the net weighing a nice 32lbs. It was a new PB, and it was a pleasure to have the biggest in my canal on my mat. After a few cheeky pics we slipped her back. Finally my target fish was caught.

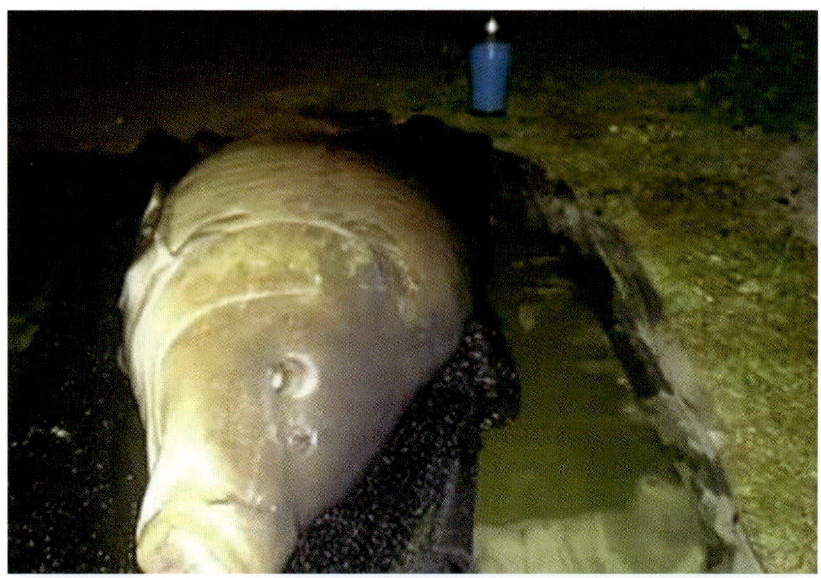

18lb common.

Nottingham Canal Carping

By Darren 'Spud' Leeman

Last September I decided to move house to get closer to my local river, the Trent, and the canal that runs through the centre of my home town, Nottingham. All the way to Grantham there are miles and miles of water to go at, and I was very exited to see what actually swam in there after hearing a few rumours here and there. Many months went by, and after work I'd walk down the canal and see if I could see any signs of carp. I did find handfuls of fish and started to put a bit of bait in but not really fishing, just watching and waiting for my chance.

One area I picked was not really on the top of my list, but I thought I would have a go, as something was just telling me to give it a try. It had all the key features: overhanging trees, moored boats and a lock, and not one carp angler in sight. Perfect! I baited an inside margin I found at 4ft deep onto a clear spot with P and B Baits Smoked Mussel and Orange boilies and some large 20mm pellets to avoid the bream if there were any present. I

then fished short evening sessions, and on the second session the rod came to life with my PB and first 20 at 29lb 3oz and my first ever canal carp! It was a very special moment in my life and one I'll never forget it!

I caught it using Korda Safe Zone leader, 3oz gripper lead mounted to a 25lb Nash combo link hook link tied to a size 6 Drennan Continental boilie hook with a smoked mussel boilie on the hair topped with a piece of fake corn and a few freebies thrown over the top. It doesn't take kilos and kilos of bait to catch a monster carp; that's what I've learnt. Just get the location right, and that's half the battle. I can't wait to get back out there!

Stainforth and Keadby Canal, Thorne, Doncaster

By Jamie Howarth

A few years ago I decided to embark upon a canal campaign. After many hours walking the Stainforth and Keadby canal, I decided upon a spot that looked like it would hold some fish – overhanging trees and mussel beds surrounded with lily pads on a bend.

It looked the best spot for miles. I began prebaiting with a mixture of fishmeal boilies, chickpeas, nuts and seeds to try and hold them in the area, as the carp in this stretch are very nomadic and holding them is key. Every couple of days I introduced around 3-4kg of mixed bait on the spot. I started fishing one or two overnighters per week, and after hundreds of bream, on my tenth night I managed to hook into something that definitely wasn't a bream. The fish flat-rodded me and put up hell of a scrap before it managed to get to the back of the overhanging tree.

After a few patient moments I managed to free it, and up it popped on the surface and into the net it went. I was buzzing. The fish weighed 21lb 2oz, and I doubt it had ever seen a hook before.

Chapter 5
Cheshire Canal

Canal Capers

By Lee Colford

For as long as I can remember I have had an association with my local canal, from drowning maggots with my dad and uncles to night fishing for bream, staring out from under a 45in brolly at the nightlights till the sun came up. During these night sessions I would often hook a carp that would make a mockery of my light lines and small hooks; an obsession with these fish was just beginning. My friend Joe and I, as well as a few others, turned our attention to trying to catch the carp that this two-mile stretch of disused Cheshire canal had to offer. We enjoyed plenty of success and had some memorable times, but it was a few years before I got amongst some of the larger specimens…

My first twenty…

It was a scorching day as Joe, Paul and I made our way to the canal. With a rod each and a loaf of Warbutons' finest, the tactics were simple: free-lined bread cast at any carp we saw, and hope it was hungry.

We took our time, looking under any likely overhangs and around snags, and it wasn't long before we saw what we were looking for. We had just come to a slight bend in the canal where the width narrowed when we noticed a common carp around halfway across. It didn't have a care in the world and just casually swam down the length of the canal with us following along. First Joe then Paul attempted to entice it by flicking crust in its path, but it just kept meandering along without even noticing. Thinking fast, I snapped a small twig from the bushes and tied it on at a depth of a few inches, then proceeded to mould a lump of bread around my size 8 hook.

I quickened my pace to get ahead of the carp and gently cast in the route it was heading. Without deviating it sucked in the bread first time, at which point I struck and all hell broke loose. It immediately headed for the fallen trees of the far bank, thrashing around as it was hooked so close to the surface. I managed to halt the initial run, and then it gave in quite quickly and was soon in the net. We quickly weighed it at 20lb exactly, and I was over the moon. It was my first 20lb'er and a new PB. Despite us trying for a few hours more no more carp were caught that day, but we

were all still buzzing at my new PB. The lads were also made up for me, making it just that bit more special to share.

Red-letter day…

Now around 22 years old, I had a young daughter and my fishing time was getting less with the extra responsibilities, although the fire was burning stronger than ever. I had managed to get a 24-hour session planned and was soon rolling along the canal on my bike, looking for some carp to target. It wasn't long before I found what I was looking for, as I noticed a couple of carp hanging around an overhanging tree enjoying the early May sun.

I quickly headed home and sorted my gear. As the canal is only a stone's throw from my house, I loaded the barrow and made the short walk there. Both rods were set up with simple pop-up rigs and Solar "Jacko Specials", my hookbait of choice. I under-armed the rods at either side of the overhang and spread a handful of boilies around each before setting up the rest of my gear for the night ahead.

I was only sat down for five minutes before the right hand rod signalled a take. I was on it quickly, and after a very typical arm-wrenching battle the carp was in the net. I was off the mark with a 17lb ghostie.

The rod was redone the same as before, and I sat back down happy to have caught one so soon. Not twenty minutes later the same rod was away again. This fish I could tell was bigger; it used its weight to hug the bottom just going left to right then back again. After a while the leadcore slowly raised from the water as a big mirror came in to view, and gulping air it went in the net first time. I quickly sorted it out, and on the scales it went 25lb and a few ounces. Buzzing! It was a lovely dark mirror, and my cousin just happened to be walking the canal and did the honours with the camera.

A little while later my friends Paul and Mike came up to see me and soon after, the right hand rod was away again! I could tell this was a smaller fish, but as my mates were there I played it cool and took my time, only for the other rod to start going too! I quickly struck and handed the rod to Mike whilst I bullied the little common into the net. Leaving Paul to sort it out I took the rod back from Mike and proceeded to do battle once again. This was obviously another larger specimen, as it stayed close to the bottom using its weight. A good ten minutes of stalemate occurred before the leadcore rose quickly, followed by the head of a large mirror as it rolled before heading back down to the bottom. Mike suddenly alerted me that it was the "30". Although I had seen it too I had tried to ignore the fact, but suddenly I had to get it in NOW! Again it rose to the surface and thankfully, gulping air, it stayed there, going in the net first time. We left her there to rest while I had a quick pic with the small common.

By now a small audience of walkers and bikers had gathered on the towpath, and as we lifted her to the unhooking mat we were subject to the usual expletives from the shocked onlookers at there being such a large fish in the canal. She weighed in at 34lb exactly, a new PB. As I held her aloft for the camera, the strain started to tell from the two fights in quick succession and four in the last few hours.

Once we had slipped her back I insisted that Mike and Paul went and got their gear as well as a few cans to celebrate. I lost another just as they

returned and that was the last of my action, although Mike helped himself to an old looking 24lb mirror. What a session, what a place!

For my good friend Joe:

Besides the sessions mentioned, my friend Joe and I had some fantastic fishing together on the canal. But as we grew older we got into other things and wouldn't go as often, with me even stopping for a year or so. It was during this break that Joe tragically took his own life.

My work at the time meant I was travelling along the canal regularly and the memories would all come flooding back. This was the catalyst for me to reignite my passion for carp fishing and the canal. One of the targets Joe and I always had was to catch one of the 20lb-plus ghosties that resided there. I felt it would be a fitting tribute to my friend to continue this quest.

It was a freezing cold February morning, and I was making my way to the area I had noticed a few carp knocking about the day before. Having put a bit of bait in I was hoping they would be up for a little feed. I got to the area and put out both rods on chod rigs with Amber Strawberry pop-ups.

Twenty minutes or so later I noticed Jezza making his way towards me to fish. At that moment my right hand rod let out a series of bleeps, and the hanger pulled up tight to the blank. I was on it quickly and proceeded to do battle with my unseen assailant as I noticed Jezza picking up his pace to come lend a hand. There was no need to rush though, as the fight was very much a slow affair, and when the fish finally neared the surface there was no mistaking it was a rather large ghostie! GULP.

At that moment I began rabbiting all sorts as I went to pieces, with Jezza trying his best to keep me calm. A few minutes later it took a big gulp of air as Jezza expertly netted it. I unhooked it and let Jezza take over the weighing. At 25lb 4oz, not only had I achieved my and Joe's goal, but I had done it in style. As I held it for Jezza to take some pics, I couldn't help think that Joe was up there smiling down on us; it was a very emotional moment for me.

I have continued to fish the canal and have had many a great time, but with the building of a new multi-lane bridge that goes over the canal it is about to undergo some massive changes. Already a long stretch of towpath has been closed, and as the project develops I fear things will only get worse. Luckily there's another canal not too far away that doesn't see much in the way of carp anglers, and I have already managed to catch a scarred-up old common on my first trip, with hopefully more to come.

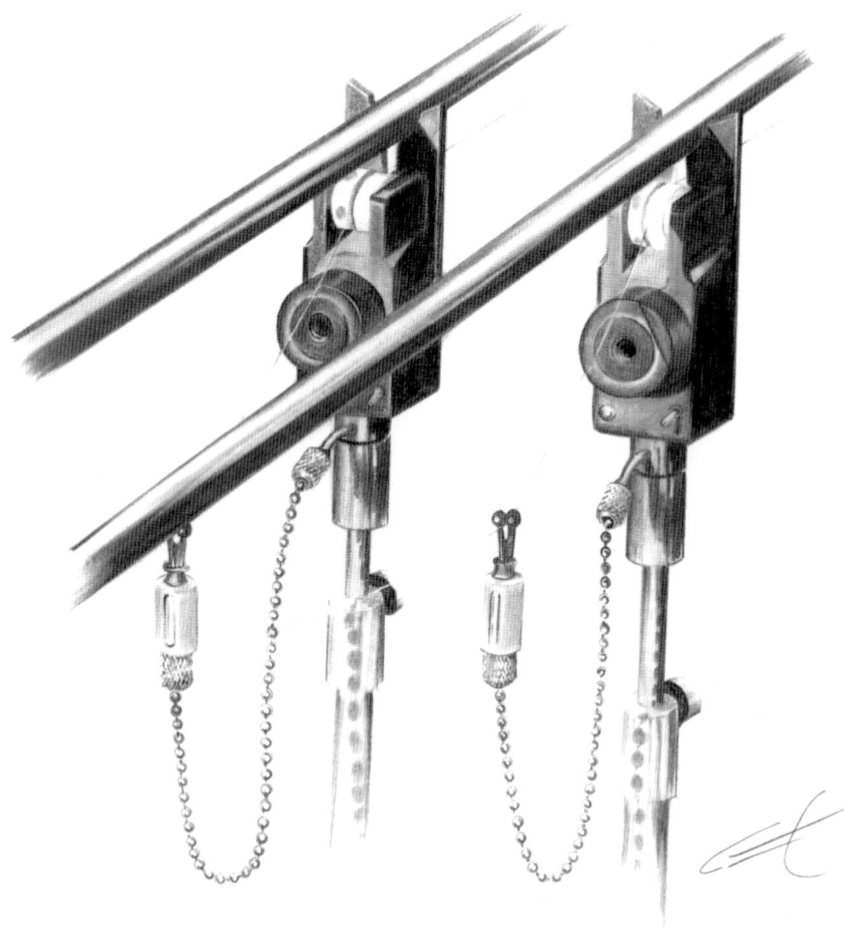

Chapter 6

The Dudley Canal

The Black Country Cut

By Josh Myatt

I started back on the canal or the "cut" as I know it, being based in the Black Country. I've fished it for as long as I can remember. The roach and perch became too little for me, and I wanted a bigger challenge. At that point I was after the tench and pike, as the carp were just myths, as I'd never seen one myself. I soon headed towards the match fishing scene, and the canal became a distant memory. Around four years later after a successful match fishing career, the stress and the rush of match fishing left me not enjoying my fishing. I'd just left school, and I decided to go in search of the carp.

I can still remember the first one I saw on this quiet little canal stretch, a mirror, and a fully scaled at that; this fish looked huge to me at the time. Now I'm guessing it was probably a mid-double, and ironically I think I've caught this fish. Soon after I spotted a common, so I ran back to grab the rods. The setup was conceived of an old Dawia Harrier 1.75tc and a small Daiwa reel. The old baitrunner has still landed me some or my biggest fish to date! To cut a long story short, I managed a take with some floating bread only to pull the hook out of the fish's mouth. I struggled that whole year for a bite, only managing two another fish on some float-fished meat. I soon met an angler pursuing the canal's hidden gems, and his name was Neil. I'd never really spoken to a carp angler at the time, as we matchmen always made them out to be horrible people. How wrong we were! Neil talked me through what he was doing and how he fished the canal and even managed an 18lb common that night!

So I kept in touch with Neil, as he was always around the area fishing, whilst trying to catch one of the canal's largest residents that we know of, the Ghostie, a fish that's now knocking on towards 30lb! I'd managed to pester the old girl for a cheap Argos setup for my birthday, and after four night sessions I finally managed my first canal fish, all 10lb 1oz of mirror. From there I started to catch of a good amount of fish in my first season. I managed 22 fish up to a 20lb 8oz mirror and a common at 20lb 4oz, which was a new PB.

Now to bring you up to date on my canal adventures… I was still doing the odd night on the canals using them as backup waters for when the parks were too busy. It was a Friday evening, and I'd just arrived and set up in a busy town spot. I'd managed to hide myself away in the trees, and there were carp present in the area, cruising under my feet. On the far bank were plenty of dog walkers and horse riders, and cyclists came rushing by on the towpath side. The day passed quickly watching fish dropping down on the spot, picking up a bait or two and then carrying on their journey. All too soon it was dark, and I sat there with coffee in hand thinking about what I'd been told by a friend, Rob, about a huge common that had been sighted in the area. It did get me wondering where it had been hiding all this time and why nobody had owned up to catching it, but I soon drifted off to sleep.

Sometime around 1:05am I awoke to three bleeps. My first thought was that it was one of the canal's pesky bream. I slowly got out of the bag and slipped my shoes on. Upon turning the head torch on, I realised my rod

Twisting and turning in the water, reflections of silver scales shining back under the moonlight.

was completely bent, as I'd forgotten to set my drag! I quickly grabbed the rod and proceeded to play the fish. What a fight it was in the clear water! The fish was twisting and turning in the water, reflections of silver scales shining back under the moon light. I knew it felt like a decent fish, but it wasn't until I put the torch on it that I realised it was a new canal PB. On seeing the torch the fish made a huge run, which left me shaking like jelly. In the end she was mine, and I recognised the fish almost instantly from the tail. It was the common I'd caught all those years back! A fish that was my first twenty was now my first 30. For the record she went 30lb 6oz, a canal thirty! Such a rare thing to find, and all on a quick overnighter. I was soon on the blower to some friends to organise pictures at first light.

I'd recently been nosing around an old stretch of the canal at one of the local boatyards. They always hold fish because of the heat off the boat in the spring and the offerings from the people living on them. It's the perfect habitat for the carp: free food, shelter and heat. I've always found my canal fish to come off small beds of bait; I've never had much luck prebaiting. I've had more luck dropping into spots after finding the fish and catching a few over a handful of bait down the edges.

Upon arrival for a quick overnighter, I'd found three fish milling around under the surface, making the most of the dying spring sun. I quickly dropped a basic pop-up rig onto a small clear spot in the weed. The night passed very quickly, as I'd had a busy day at work the day before with just a single bleep in the night being all that disturbed me. I was awoken by another single bleep, this time around 6am, and I decided to slip my shoes on and check my spots. As I moved closer I could see a little white pop-up being thrown about in the water. Confused and half asleep, it took me a moment to realise there was a dark shape attached to my rig, shaking its head violently. I quickly ran back to my rods and the water exploded with a huge vortex.

There were massive lunges and boat dodging as the fish was trying to cut me off, using the boat as a snag. All of a sudden everything came to a halt. I presumed the fish had "done the off" with the hook, but I still decided to net the huge ball of weed that was close to 4ft long. That's when I laid my eyes on the prettiest fish I'd ever seen; it was like unwrapping a

Don't underestimate the forgotten, underfished places. Sometimes they hold the biggest surprise.

present as a kid on Christmas morning. As I pushed the weed aside, the longest, darkest linear appeared. What a fish she was! I'd heard rumours of a large mirror being in the area, and once again by dropping into an area for no more than 12 hours, I'd managed to snag her on just a handful of bait. I'd caught this fish several years before, my first one off a floater when I first started for them, at 17lb 10oz. This time she tipped the scales at 27lb 8oz. It's great to meet an old friend once again and to see her in immaculate condition, and she'd grown a lot in five years. I rang a friend to come and do the pictures, and I'll let you have a look at those.

The Dudley Canal System

By Darren Dunn and Anthony Williamson

Here are a few of our canal carp out of the Dudley canal system. We have been watching these carp for a while now and decided to wet a line for them. We baited up for a few days, first with a mixture of particles and boilies. First session we had three carp to 18lb, which we were over the moon with. Two sessions later a 27lb 11oz mirror and a 25lb 1oz had graced

27lb 11oz.

14lb 10oz.

25lb 1oz.

18lb 4oz.

14lb 2oz.

our nets. In total we have had 11 carp varying from 10lb up to the big one. The fish are all in mint condition, and to see people's faces as we pull them out is a picture.

Urban Legends...

Tales Of Whispered Monsters By Craig McEvoy

My passion for urban monsters was lit quite early in my life, way back in the days that I was still a young pup at junior school actually! There was a place that was about a ten-minute walk from my house that was an old hospital sanatorium. In the hospital grounds was a large, deep pool surrounded by woodland. Rumours told that the hospital used to use it to dispose of chemicals, medicines, waste and even the occasional dead patient! Well, as a kid you believed anything, and my imagination used to run wild with stories of monster fish lurking in the deep, dark depths of the lake, mutating on the medicines and feeding on the flesh of humans! It was a scary place for a young Black Country lad!

One year the pool had filled with water so much that on one rain filled summer's day it broke free from its banks, and the rushing waters meandered straight into the side tributary that linked to the canal at the back of the pool. It wasn't long before stories made their way to my ears of unseen beasts that had escaped the depths of the sanatorium pool into the canal, smashing match anglers' tackle to pieces. I begged and begged my mum for weeks to take me down the local "cut", as to a poor Black Country eight-year-old, opportunities to catch such fish were virtually nonexistent.

Eventually one Sunday afternoon she reluctantly agreed, and we made our way down to the canal. I remember the walk to the canal as though it was yesterday. The excitement bubbling away inside me; I had never felt such excitement... well, except maybe for when Santa was due on Christmas Eve! We got to the canal, and I remember there being a few old guys fishing. I put down my wicker basket and began putting my old fibreglass rod together. It was a heavy old thing that was naturally bent with the weight of the actual rod. The reel was a lovely original Mitchell match reel bought for me one Christmas by my uncle Norman, and it was attached to the rod with two sliding metal rings.

I soon had a float on the line and tied a hook on with a six-turn blood knot that my uncle had showed me. I hooked on a piece of bread and flicked out the float, ever so gracefully, and watched in horror as my reel came away from the rod and landed in the oily waters of the canal! I burst into tears as my reel disappeared into the depths of the cut. I pulled and pulled at the line but all that happened was more and more line got pulled from the reel, until I had a right old birds nest of Maxima next to me on the towpath. Mom didn't have a clue what to do, but luckily the old guy from up the towpath saw what was going on and came down to help. He had a Y shaped rod rest, and he proceeded to follow the line from the rod into the margins of the canal and managed to hook the bail arm of the reel and fish out the reel for me!

I was so happy! He smiled, and like some sort of magician, out of his pocket, he pulled out two pieces of bicycle inner tube and proceeded to slide them up the rod butt. He then attached my reel, sliding the inner tube over the reel, securing it firmly to the rods. He winked at me and said, "'Ere you are, lad, you won't lose your reel anymore." And with that he handed me my rod and reel and made his way back to his blue plastic Shakespeare seat box.

I continued to fish... well, more like fly fish, as I spent more time reeling in and casting out than fishing. I must have looked more like a lure fisherman than a coarse fisherman... well, boy! The next thing I remember will live with me forever and was the catalyst to the fire that still burns strongly inside me to this day! "I'm in, Bob!" I heard, and as I looked up the towpath, there was the helpful old guy stood up, rod in hand with it bent double. My mum and I watched in awe as an amazing battle commenced. The unseen monster, on the other end of his line, tore off up and down the centre channel of the canal. If I close my eyes, I can still hear his screaming drag from his tortured old reel! The old guy held on for dear life, his rod creaking as it engaged in battle. Soon a big black back broke the surface oil of the canal, and he quickly scooped his net around it.

I ran up the bank to see what he had caught, with mom calling after me, but I had to see it! He laid the monster on the grass next to the towpath and parted the mesh. He held her up for me, and her scales lit up beautifully in the afternoon sunshine. He smiled... "There you go, son. That's what lives in here – a bloody big carp!" At that he returned her to her watery home, and little did he know that he had just started something within me that would live with me forever, and some 27 years later, that passion still burns away as brightly as it ever has.

Ever since that day I have been fascinated with carp and carp fishing, but I have always had a soft spot for a bit of canal carping. I have walked many, many miles trying to catch these marauding urban legends, and every so often I get lucky and land an urban monster. Let me talk you through some of the more memorable moments from the "cut" and try to help you, the reader, catch your own urban legend!

Doing Your Homework

My first bit of advice I can give to anyone is to buy the angling weeklies, scour the Internet and walk the canals talking to the match guys. Look out for any information on carp catches or more so of big fish being lost. This will give you the heads up of stretches that contain carp. It is also worth sharing information with people, as they are more likely to disclose information to you if you help them with their current target.

A few years back I helped a young lad with fishing a large undisclosed gravel pit and disclosed a few secrets to him that helped him go on and catch his PB. In return he told me of a stretch of canal that contained fish in excess of 30lb and even sent me the photos to prove it! This information alone led me to catch my PB canal carp of 35lb 6oz! Now for the important bit... When you find a stretch that contains these monsters, you will need to do everything in your power to keep it to yourself. This includes where you have your trophy shot taken! It's amazing how many would-be detectives are out there, and they will blow up your images and look for any clue that will give the location of your capture away. I learned the hard way, and the location of my big common was soon discovered, as the next time I turned up, the banks were lined with Brotels and matching rods! It looked like a scene from Linear Fisheries, and when I spoke to the guys, they had noticed graffiti on the bridge and a blue covered fence. They knew roughly the area I was fishing, so had walked the towpath until they found the spot that matched the picture. Good angling, but I was gutted. Lesson learnt, I soon took the picture down off my Facebook page, but the horse had already bolted. Luckily I knew of several stretches that contained rather large carp, and I would never make that same mistake again. When fishing the canal I have made several observations that are worth noting and will aid you in your quest.

Elusive Nomads

Firstly, location... Canal carp are notoriously nomadic and can roam miles and miles of canal. However from my experience the fish will be in different places along the canal at different times of year. In winter look towards the marinas and areas of a high population of boats. Not any boats, but preferably boats that are lived on. These provide warmth, cover and regular food from the people that live on the boats.

Winter – A great tip in winter is to walk the canal when the weather is really cold, and I mean really cold. The canal should be frozen solid. Walk its banks and look for areas that are not frozen, as this will give an indication of warmer water, and the carp will congregate in these areas in the winter. In fact by doing this I have found a stretch of canal that has a water treatment plant next to it that pumps in warm water through the winter. The result is a section of the canal that can be fished in any conditions and produces sport all winter long! Most of my canal fishing now takes part in the winter when every other water has shut up shop. But if you can find areas like these and ones that still see regular boat traffic or boats that are lived on, you may just have a winter to remember.

Spring – In spring I always look for tree cover and shallower water in close proximity to the winter holding spots. These will be the first spots to be visited after the long harsh winter, as the carp seek out the warm rays of the spring sunshine, but they will prefer some sort of cover to feel confident. I know of an area that lies about 200yds up from a marina that has a large overhanging tree and is 3ft shallower than the rest of that stretch, and it is here where I will visit in the spring to catch a canal monster or two! In fact I have taken several 20s from this spot!

Summer – Look for the dead arms / quiet areas, as the carp will pack into these areas to rest up and get out the way of the busy boat traffic. I

Warm water entering the canal creating a winter oasis.

One off the top – an opportunity that came about after a countryside meal and drink with family and friends… Always keep a rod handy.

A perfect winter spot.

have found up to 30 carp in an arm no more than 10yds wide and 30yds long. Here the water will be still and perfect for a bit of floater fishing.

Overhanging trees are also another favourite haunt of the carp in summer, and a bait placed close to these stands a good chance of being taken. Especially look for stretches that have large areas of no cover or features and has only one tree on its length. There will be carp here!

Inlets are another prime area to look for, as the extra oxygen will have the carp lining up in the heat of the summer. Remember a carp's prime instinct is survival, and oxygen plays a major role obviously... a much bigger role than people realise. Oxygen aids digestion and helps make the fish feels more comfortable, therefore it is more likely to feed harder in these areas and a lot more likely to make a mistake with a hookbait!

Turning points, basins... the list is endless! My biggest is advice is to get yourself a bike and a good pair of polaroids. Start prowling the canal towpaths in the summer, as this is a great time to assess carp stocks in the stretches of canal and from here you can formulate a plan. Another good tip is to try and be at the canal when spawning takes place, as this will allow you to see the size of the carp in the stretch.

Preparation Is The Key To Success!

Once your location is sorted, the next step to consider is your bait and its application. It's not simply a case of throwing in a load of boilies and then hauling them out. They may not even know what these wonderful smelling round balls are... Before you throw any bait in I suggest you follow the next bit of advice. I first pick out five spots along a stretch of canal. I will then take my marker rod with just a lead attached and donk the spots to assess the level of silt, debris, snags etc. A useful tip is to attach a bit of white string to the lead and smell this upon your retrieve. The string will tell you if the bottom is foul or presentable. Once you have found some decent spots, the next stage that I do is clear the area of any major debris that may foul presentation. I do this by clipping on a Thinking Anglers weed rake and have a few casts around the spot. This will clear the main debris of twigs and litter like carrier bags from the spot, leaving a lovely area to present a bait.

What I do next is drag the lead the length of the canal. The lead is attached to a 3lb weak link in case it snags so you can break free easily. This will identify any snags that may be present that you need to be aware of when you hook a fish. There's nothing worse than hooking a canal carp, only for it to do you in a Tesco shopping trolley or an old stolen rusty motorbike!

Right now it's time to apply the bait. I always start with using the classic combination of hemp and corn with a mixture of halibut pellets thrown in, a couple of pints of white maggots (very visual) and some crushed and whole boilie that I will be using later as my hookbaits. I apply the halibuts to the mix about 15 minutes before baiting, as this gives them time to soak in the hemp and sweetcorn juices but not long enough to turn to mush. Now for the clever bit: I add rock salt, betaine and green lipped mussel to ensure the carp are getting all the vitamins and minerals they need (especially important prior to and after spawning). I then add my chosen flavour to the mix to give it a label and to help the carp associate that flavour with food... and good highly nutritious food. This is important for the next stage of my baiting plan.

Once I have chosen my spots I first introduce this bait combo in the hope of attracting everything that swims. This does two things: firstly the feeding activity won't go unnoticed by the carp if they are near, and secondly the feeding activity will help clear your spots of any new small debris like twigs, weed and silt. I like to apply the bait over a two-week period if possible. The first week I will bait up every other day with a kilo of this mix. The second week, I drop the particle and pellet completely and switch to my chosen boilie only. My chosen bait is Squid and Tangerine from the Tor Baits stable. It is a potent, highly nutritious, fishmeal type bait that has caught me fish from all over the UK, France and Spain! The problem with canals is that they can be full of hungry bream and tench, and the particle/pellet approach will attract them like wildfire... not what you want when you're fishing for big nomadic carp. I will again bait twice with just half a kilo of boilies on each spot.

The day that I decide to fish I will have put in some bait the night before, but hardly any on the day I am fishing. I will only take a kilo of bait with me to last a whole 24-hour session. I will then spend five hours in each spot, and if I've had no action within this time frame, I will move on to my next spot. Obviously travelling light is the name of the game, so leave your two-man hotels at home!!! A fox Supa Brolly will suffice, and two rods is more than ample for the canal.

I am often asked if the effort is really worth it? I am on syndicates that hold fish in excess of 50lbs, but still nothing beats the allure for me of a big, wild urban monster. Let me recount a tale that proves my point...

Monster Of The "Cut"

It was a few years ago now when a drunken conversation in the local pub brought to my attention a tale of monster carp in the canal. Tales of 30s and even a 40 were spoken about in hushed tones. The story told of monster carp that lived in a Midland marina that couldn't be fished, but on the odd occasion they would venture out into the main canal and make a mistake...

It was a few days later that I decided to take a walk along this aforementioned canal and make my way to the marina. I know I shouldn't have, but I climbed over the fence into the marina to have a quick scout about to see if I could see anything of any interest. My first impression was one of disappointment. The marina was only very small with about six barges moored up and that made it full! It was just like a big round turning point off the main canal. I made my way to the water's edge and I froze in disbelief. My eyes bulged and were out on stalks... There basking next to one of the boats was a carp of epic proportions. It must have weighed in excess of 35lbs easily! It was a thickset black mirror that just hung there motionless, without a care in the world! From the corner of my eye it was joined by two smaller commons. All were in excess of 20lb, but the big black mirror dwarfed them. The commons were light in colour. I was feverish with excitement, and I nearly wet myself when a huge battle-scarred common made its way through the gap of the marina and out into the main canal! The common was well in excess of 30lbs, and I just couldn't believe what I was seeing! These were easily the biggest canal carp I had ever seen by some considerable margin! Suddenly I heard someone shout, "Oi! What are you up to?" As I looked around, the marina security guard was making his way over. I quickly hopped back over the fence and

My first true monster canal carp.

A baiting pole is a great edge on a canal.

made my way off up the towpath… but I knew I'd be back!

Over the next few weeks I couldn't get those fish out my mind. They occupied every thought, so a few weeks later I found myself on the towpath opposite the marina. I fished three overnighters without so much as a gudgeon farting, but at night I could hear them crashing in the marina opposite. You couldn't cast far enough into the marina, as there was a bridge that went over the entrance, just high enough for the barges to pass under. It was heartbreakingly frustrating, as I knew what was in the marina, but I couldn't get to them! I was sitting at home one night and couldn't get these canal monsters out of my mind when suddenly I had a brainwave (a rare event)…

It was my fourth visit to the "monster marina" when I put my plan into action. I arrived just on dark with my brother and cast onto the bank opposite. I slackened off my drag and made my way up to bridge, 50yds to the left of where we were set up. We crossed the bridge, and I jumped the marina fence, leaving my brother the safe side of the fence. My brother passed me the baiting pole, and I made my way to the little bridge that went over the entrance to the marina. My brother followed the fence towards the little bridge, and he quickly found my lead. He attached my rig/stick and made his way to the little bridge and waited for me. I shipped out the baiting pole under the bridge out towards the main canal. My brother put my rig and handful of Tor Baits Squid and Tangerine in the spoon and made his way back to the rods. I slowly eased the pole back under the bridge and glided it to the side of the first boat where I stealthily deposited my rig and bait right next to the boat where I had seen the monster mirror! I made my way back out the marina in full stealth mode and down over the main canal bridge to meet my brother stationed at the rods.

We sat there and giggled like two school children at our mischievousness! It took several hours and we were into our fourth brew when suddenly the tip flew round and the receiver vibrated in my pocket! I was fishing locked up with 15lb Pro Gold, and I just held on for dear life. It takes some conviction not to give any line, and my heart was in my mouth. The Fox Warrior rod was bent double and my little Shimano

Baitrunner was trying to give line, even though it was fully tightened. I clasped the spool and dipped the tip below the water. I had watched the match guys do this at Drayton reservoir to gain control of large carp on their light setups. It worked a treat, and I managed to turn her. The entrance to the marina rocked as the fish came through the gap to our side. I raised the rod, and she spent the next five minutes sending up huge boils and vortices in the torchlight. Up she rose, and we caught our first glimpse of her, a pale common that looked every inch a good 20. My legs had turned to jelly, and I just prayed the hook wouldn't pull. I needn't have worried, as a few minutes later, up she popped, and I led her over the waiting net!

"YES!" I shouted in complete ecstasy! She was mine! We peered into the net, and we could see that she was indeed a good 20. My bro sorted out the mat, scales and camera, as I was shaking from the adrenaline that was coursing through my veins. We lifted her onto the scales, and at 25lb 2oz she was my new canal PB. I was buzzing and smiling ear to ear as I held her up for the camera. She was a wonderful; almost ghostlike in colour with not a scale out of place. As I slipped her back I thanked her for making me one very happy carper! It was a fantastic feeling, and although I knew there were bigger in there, I was just so happy to have caught such a wonderful carp.

I did indeed go on to catch my first canal 30 from here on one summer's morning, but that's another story for another time. My brother is currently targeting his first canal 30 (or possibly bigger) so I can only disclose the night picture of my 25lb 2oz common, but watch this space... It just goes to show that canals do hold some truly monstrous carp! Oh and that big mirror is still there!

Safety First

One thing I must express is the importance of keeping yourself safe on the canal. Canals are not the safest of places, and you will find many unsavoury characters using them for all sorts of things. I have witnessed many things on the canal, from people casing local factories in preparation of a burglary and then later being visited by the police to see if I had seen something suspicious, to being visited by many a drunk, usually friendly but full of babble. I have seen glue sniffers under the bridges, frisky couples getting hot on the towpath, fights opposite at the closing time of a local pub, motorbikes speeding along the towpath… It's definitely not a place for the faint hearted, so please follow my safety guide to try and limit the amount of danger you may unknowingly put yourself in:

- Buy yourself some cheap rods and reels – leave the Basias and Techniums at home. Less is definitely more on the canal, and you are a lot less likely to get robbed!
- Leave a deterrent on show, so people will think twice about robbing you.
- Don't fish near to pubs or towns on the weekend when there is a much more likely chance of there being drunks using the towpaths at these times.
- Carry a mobile phone with a reliable contact on speed dial.
- Put the app "Find My iPhone" on your mobile if possible, as you never know when you may need this.
- Let someone know where you're going and likely time to return.

- Get your tackle security marked in case the worst happens.
- Never fish alone! Always fish in pairs or more.
- Always fish with the brolly facing the rods in close proximity.

If people seem to be hanging about, start having a conversation with your mate, so that they can hear, along the lines of, "Yeah the boys are coming down in a bit." This will make them think twice.

If it looks dodgy then move on… No carp is worth putting yourself in danger.

Edges

Here are a couple more tips and tricks for you all on the canal that I hope will help you land a monster of your own… Fish with a white hookbait. I don't know why, but white seems to catch a hell of a lot of marauding canal carp. Maybe it's because of the amount of bread that people throw to the ducks or off the boats? Who knows? But it is more than a coincidence! Next is to fish through the night… Yes, I know this can seem dangerous, but if you follow the safety tips described it will reduce the danger considerably! I have found on canals, especially some of the more pressured ones, that the carp have switched to feeding at night. They may have learnt that there is danger in the day, but when night falls it's safe to go on the munch… or so they thought!

Avoid chods – I have found that the tow on the canals can be considerable, and chods are just not the one! If you have cleared your spots, a simple KD rig is much, much more effective! Think about this for a second. You're fishing slack lines on the chods, but the tow is tightening your line, potentially lifting these off the bottom. At the very best they will be waving around unnaturally!

Use a baiting pole to fish under trees or next to boats. This will avoid conflict with boat owners, as they don't take kindly to a 2oz lead being thrown at their pride and joy, plus it's perfect bait placement every time!

Strong smelling baits seem to work better on the canals.

Avoid pellets when fishing unless you love bream!

Place a white bucket, a couple of yards up, either side of your rods. This prevents the bikers crashing into your setup. I have even glued reflectors on mine!

Use back leads to avoid the boat traffic – a must in the height of summer!

Do not set up next to water stops for the boats on the canals, as I nearly got into a right old fight as a boat nearly crashed into my rods.

Put your rods horizontal to the towpath to avoid walkers and bikers.

Keep a small stalking setup and some floaters in the van/car as in the summer when taking the missus and kids a walk along the canal, you never know when an opportunity might present itself!

Don't tell anyone anything, as you will be surprised at just how many sheep love the canal!

Well, I hope you've enjoyed this article and have taken away some tips that will help you to catch one of those urban legends... and remember they are catchable in the canal in any conditions!

Until next time, slack lines and screaming buzzers! Daddy Mac.

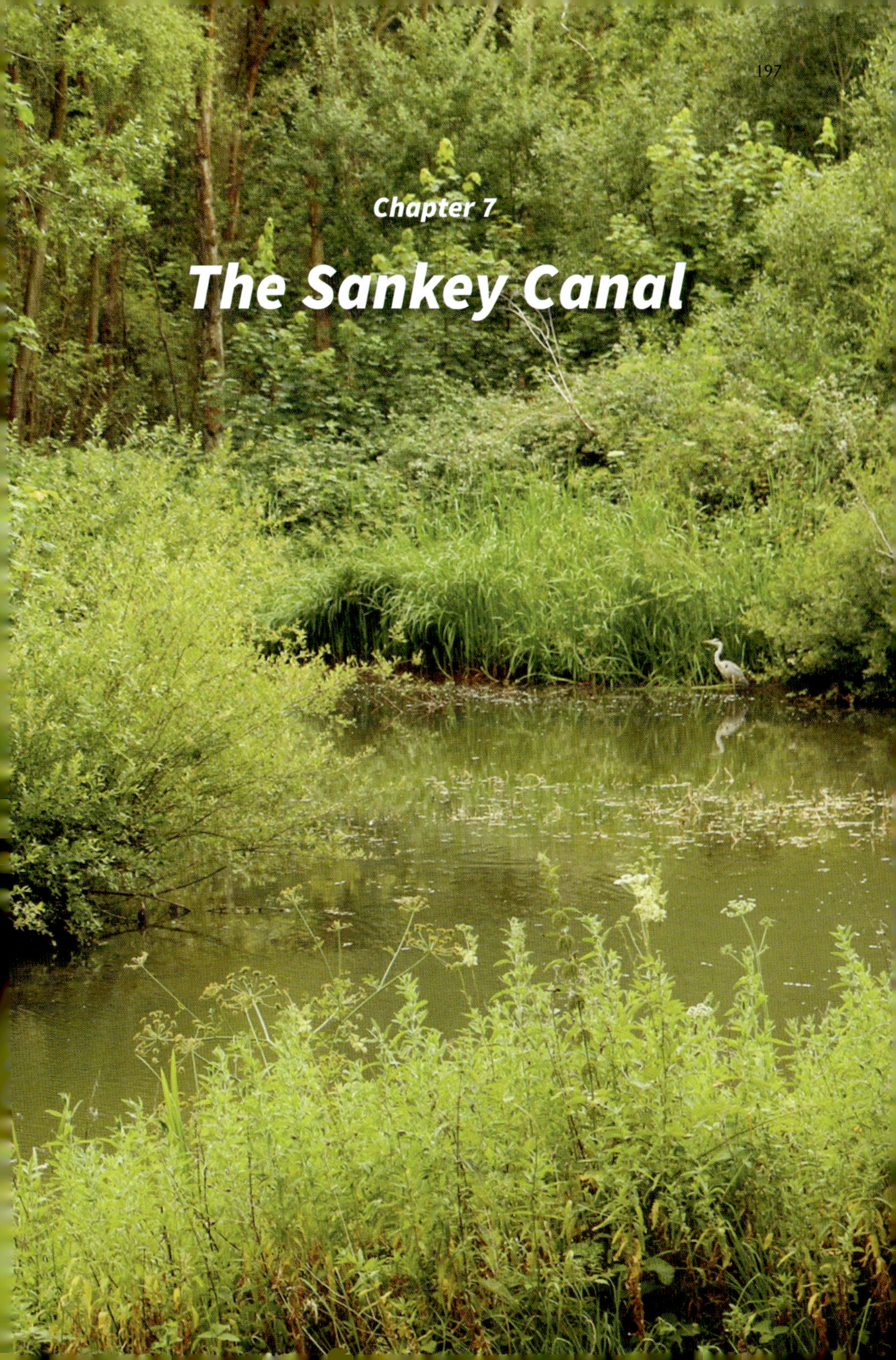

Chapter 7

The Sankey Canal

The Unstable Campaign

By Lee Colford

I don't know about you, but for me this last winter was a headbanger. I fished hard for no reward, and come the first signs of spring and my first bite for months, I only bloody lost it due to a cut off on my leader. I'd had enough, and a new challenge was needed. Thankfully I had just the place in mind. The venue is one I had done the odd trip on over the last few years, and I had picked up snippets of info from the odd angler I met, and of course the dog walkers. Plenty of you will no doubt see dog walkers as a pain at times, but who better to get info from than people who are using the towpath regularly? Obviously their perspective of fish sizes may be a little over the top, but generally the numbers they see and the areas they see them in are spot-on. If you haven't guessed yet from the towpath clue, the venue in question is a canal – not just any canal, but one that is actually disused and "closed" for angling. The reason for this is the banks are crumbling away and unstable. The local council has erected long stretches of fencing preventing you from getting to the water's edge along a lot of it, although there are a few places to get the rods out.

After the loss of my first bite in months it was soon half term for the kids, so for a couple of weeks the rods would be gathering dust. I put this time to good use though; in fact it probably worked out better, as I took my time to pick an area and get the bait going in. Over the half term I made the nine-mile round trip on my bike four times, each time emptying a bucket of hemp, tares, tigers and Excelsor boilies from Beechwood Baits over the area. I was buzzing for it on the few days leading up to my first trip. On all my recce trips I had yet to see another angler, but had seen a few carp. Empty banks and rarely caught carp – I was looking forward to this! I decided to start off by just fishing short evening sessions, arriving around 7:30pm after riding there from home and fishing through till 1am before riding home again. A lot of effort, but I was sure it would be worth it.

Friday dragged, as it always does when you're watching the clock, waiting for that magic time when you can leave the world behind and go fishing. The journey there was trouble free, and I made good time in spite of the nonstop rain. I was all set up by 8pm and was happy with how it was all going. Around 9:10pm the right hand rod bent round, and I was in! The fish put up a short but spirited fight in the fading light. As I drew it over the net I couldn't quite believe my eyes! Over the last few years I had heard the tales from the dog walkers and the occasional angler about the big golden koi, but never had I actually seen it. Yet here it was staring back at me! It went 12lb, but honestly, who cares? After a few pics I returned it and got the rod back out. I was just in the process of sending a few quick messages when once again the recast rod was away! I was liking it here already. Another spirited but short fight ensued, and a lovely old looking 11lb 4oz mirror had me smiling from ear to ear. It was just gone 10pm when I had the rod back out, but seeing as I had already been blessed with a lovely brace of fish I decided to give it till 11:30pm then depart earlier than planned. As it happens it was a good decision, and I flew home on my bike that night. Before I left though, I deposited half a bucket of hemp, tares, tigers and Excelsor over the area.

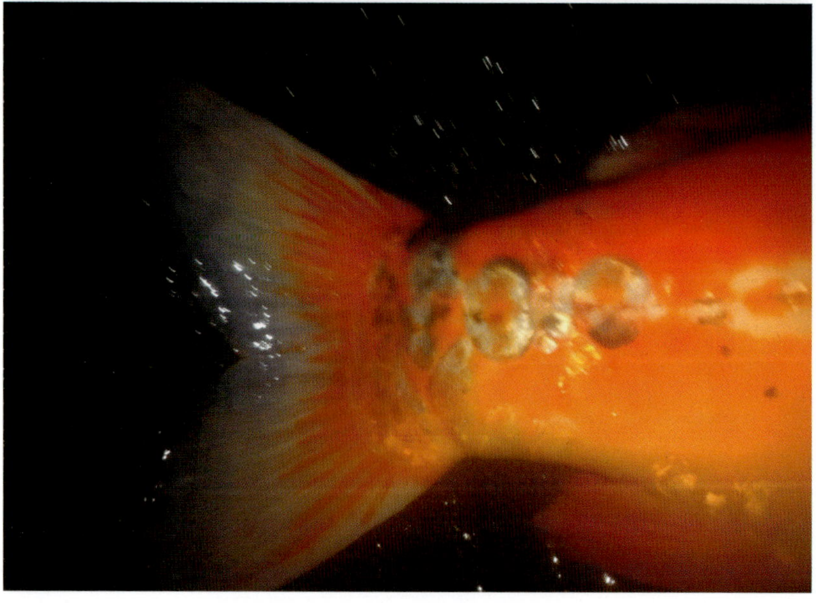

On my return the following evening it was a simple case of flicking the rods back out with just a handful of Excelsor and tigers around each. It was looking good with the odd fish showing in the area, maybe tench, but with the sun out and not a spot of rain like the previous evening, I was more than happy. Again I didn't have too long to wait, and just before 9pm I had a take. This time the left hand rod was the one to go, and instantly it felt a better fish than the two the previous evening. It tried hard to find sanctuary in the reed bed, but thankfully walking backwards got it away before it put up a good fight under the tip. As it popped up for netting my jaw hit the floor, as a huge mouth and head neared the net with large scales adorning its side. I scooped it up quickly, and instantly dropped the rod to take in the beautiful scaly creature I had been blessed to catch. What a fish! I let out a little victory cry to myself whilst securing the net and getting the mat and camera ready. It looked even better as it lay glistening on the mat in the fading sun; I was truly buzzing! For the record it went 19lb 12oz, but I really couldn't care! Feeling blessed with my two short evening successes I decided to leave at 10:30pm and again give them a free meal and not push my luck too soon in the campaign.

I had a few beers that night once home, and they tasted ever so sweet after a blank winter, I can tell you.

The following Wednesday I again rode up and give them a good hit of the bait mix. I couldn't wait for Friday evening to come around again.

Friday arrived a little earlier after a bit of sweet-talking to the missus; the pull was already getting strong. It was looking good, and I had a quick lead about on the spot to see if it was getting clearer, and it certainly was. What was once dying weed and sticky silt had become much cleaner, and the lead slid along the bottom. Unfortunately I spooked one on my first cast! I got the rods sorted the same as last week and was confident of a bite as the reeds were knocking like crazy. I was thinking after an hour or so that I should have had one, but put it down to overconfidence because of my results the previous weekend. I figured they would trip up eventually, so I sat on my hands. How wrong! I left it till 9:30pm before it got the better of me, and on retrieving the rod that had seen the most activity around it, I noticed it was tangled! A wasted few hours there, but I live and

DANGER
Unstable
canal wall
No angling

learn. I had been using the other rod as a roaming rod, trying a different spot with minimal bait just as a contrast to the heavily prebaited area, but it didn't produce either. By 11pm the activity had ceased, so I put out another good hit of bait and left for home, a lesson learnt and noted. Also the old weed had come up and was floating around everywhere making line lay a little difficult at times. Another problem to solve, but I figured it was coming, and already a solution to this problem was ready to go.

I only had the one evening session that weekend, so that was it till the week after. I planned on doing a full night next time and try to get the evening and dawn bite times into play.

I couldn't make it back to fish for a fortnight, but I carried on with the baiting. Every three days I made the journey on my bike; I was racking up some miles, that's for sure. I baited with a bucket full of the same mix of hemp, tares, tiger nuts and Excelsor boilies every time. My last trip to bait up was earlier in the day than previous baiting trips. It meant I had a chance of spotting anything, whereas before, I was getting in and out quickly on dusk, which didn't give me much chance of fish spotting. To be honest it wasn't till I was making to leave after baiting that I spotted anything, and it was only another koi! This one was white with black and orange markings. I had never been told or heard anything about this one. I'm guessing they have come from the local housing estate after outgrowing their owner's pond. God knows what else could be in there.

Thankfully I had managed to arrange a lift for the weekend. Plans were afoot to do a full night, so with any luck the baiting would have worked its magic, and I would get amongst them again.

I arrived for my overnighter at 9:20pm and quickly got the rods out. I had just laid the bedchair out when I noticed in the distance two fluorescent yellow jackets heading my way down the towpath. Ah shit... Was I about to be told to pack up and go home by the police? I sat down and didn't do anything but watch as they got closer and closer. As they approached I nodded in their direction and said, "Evening". They replied with an "Evening" of their own and carried on walking! I guess I was worrying for nothing, ha ha! All was quiet till around 3am when I had a bream-like occurrence on the left hand rod. I took my time, put my shoes

on and casually walked to the rod. Upon picking it up it hooped over, and a carp rolled on the surface. I had a little trouble with the ever-increasing weed clinging to the line. It was making it difficult to net, but in it went eventually, and a 21lb 14oz ghostie was my prize. My first twenty of the year, and the fish were gradually getting bigger from the spot. Nothing else occurred, and I was packed up and heading for home by 10am.

I again baited the spot through the week and fished it on the Friday night but no joy. I got a feeling they had moved off to spawn somewhere. What with the good weather the previous week, it seems they were waiting for it. I stuck some more bait on it before I left though and planned to keep it going in through the following week, but not planning to fish it. I thought giving them a few free meals without pressure could pay off after their yearly ritual. I rode up to bait it again on the Wednesday. Just as I was finishing a guy came along who said he had been fishing it a little further up for the past month or so! (Rumbled!!). It was quite clear to him I had been baiting, and I had also cleared weed from the front of the swim with the rake. The way he came across, I could imagine him jumping on it. Time would tell I guess, but I had a feeling this could be the beginning of the end. I would go back up to bait again Saturday evening, and I would be able to tell if my peg has been trodden or not. My next trip fishing I had penciled in for a Wednesday day session. After that I decided to make the call to either carry on or leave it be. The weed was now up to the surface along most of the stretch, and my spot was quite obvious, just a 12ft wide gap in the weed from bank to bank with large piles of weed on the bank from my raking efforts to keep it fishable.

Saturday I went to stick some more bait on the spot, and lo and behold I came across the "other" koi. I managed a quick pic on my phone before he disappeared under the weed. I was getting an itch for the need to catch me this fish. On the plus side the swim had looked untouched from the guy who rumbled me on Wednesday, so all was good at the minute. I planned to stick another small bucket in on Tuesday then fish a day on Wednesday. Just to add, the koi wasn't the only carp I saw that day.

I Arrived around 9am on Wednesday and was fishing in double quick time due to getting everything ready the night before. I had made the effort to get back up the previous day and just top up the spot a little in preparation. With the weed the way it was, there was no real way of fish spotting in the area, and honestly, it wasn't looking good. I'm not one to waste my sessions, so at 1pm I was off and heading for the area I had seen the other koi hanging around. Due to not knowing how clear the area was of weed, I switched over to chods. An hour later I had my first bite. Due to the nature of the ground where I had set up, my rod butts were resting on a bucket. The rod went flying on the take, but thankfully I was on it quickly. Instantly it locked up in weed, and I was left winding it in, not sure if the carp was still attached. Trying to net it all was a pain; the first time I thought I had it all only to notice my line sticking out of the net with a carp still attached. I dropped everything and started ripping off the weed, and in it popped second time around, and a stunning little common of around 9lb was my prize. What it lacked in size it certainly made up for in looks; it was scale perfect and black as coal, so I was more than pleased.

An hour later the left hand rod was away, and after a good scrap and no drama from the weed, my second of the day was in the net – this time a mirror with large fins, big scales and again lovely dark colour. It probably weighed around 13lb but I didn't weigh it; I really didn't care. All the while the other koi was hanging around the area, teasing me by staying close to the surface despite the rain. I switched one rod to a zig and put it on the patrol route I had seen him using, but to no avail. I packed up and rode home at 5pm, happy that I had made the move and got the most from my session.

With the weed now at its

worst I've decided to call an end to it... for now. I may go back in the autumn to see what else lurks beneath the surface, or to try and get my picture taken with the "other" koi, but for now I've got other plans. Over the period of time I undertook this campaign, I rode, for baiting up and fishing, somewhere in the region of 140 miles and only put in around 50 total fishing hours. All this around a busy family life, it just goes to prove that effort can equal reward! I'm in need of a break, so I may just go back to the local to exorcise the demons of that blank winter and try and catch a few chunks.

Chapter 8

The South Holland Main Drain

South Holland Main Drain Carp

By Liam Chapman

As in most venues during the winter months the carp become less active and shoal up in larger groups. It had got to mid November, and my syndicate water near Peterborough had really slowed down. It's very shallow, so it does tend to switch off fairly quickly as soon as the temperatures start to plummet. I also fish my local drain, the Holland, throughout the season anyway, doing the odd evening after work fishing until dark (night fishing isn't allowed).

So as we got to late autumn I had a good idea of where the fish would be held up, as my brother Leigh and I kept the zone topped up with Raw Baits Nutex boilies three times a week, then fished that area on a Saturday or a Sunday. All the fair-weather anglers seemed to have put away their rods for the winter, so if we could keep the fish in the area we knew we could catch a few without being seen, and avoid anyone else uninvited joining the party!

From mid November until early December we managed 20 fish between us, all commons to 23lb 8oz. The Drainage Board then dredged the river, and this moved the fish elsewhere. It proved very difficult to find them after that, so we split up and fished different stretches to try and locate them, but the ice cold mornings seem to hit you harder when you're

RAW
NUTEX
Precision Engineered Bait
14
18
www.rawbaits.com
NUTEX

OCEAN

OCEAN
OCEAN

not catching or seeing any signs of fish!

Christmas and New Year soon came and went, and early February we decided to have a go one morning where a friend reckoned he'd seen one nudge out as he drove home on the way back from football on a Sunday lunchtime the previous week. Washed out Nutex pop-ups were flicked out, and within minutes I was getting savage liners... A couple of hours had passed without any more action, and I began to wonder if I'd been imagining the knocks and pulls on the rod tips earlier on. Finally the right-hander slammed round and a fish started taking line. A mid double ghostie was quickly unhooked, photographed and returned. I then put in around a kilo of Nutex boilies in before I left, as Leigh was going to fish the following afternoon.

I stopped by on the way home from work in a torrential hailstorm to see how he was doing. He'd only been fishing 45 minutes and had one in the net whilst playing another! He managed four fish from five bites in three hours' fishing, which is awesome for February in such Arctic conditions!

We fished that area again with regular baiting every few days throughout February until early March and had 18 carp between us in short afternoon trips. The slight flow of the river helps keep the carp more active than they are in lakes during the colder months. If they're using energy they need to refuel, so you can give them plenty of bait! We'll certainly be back this winter for another go... Tight lines!

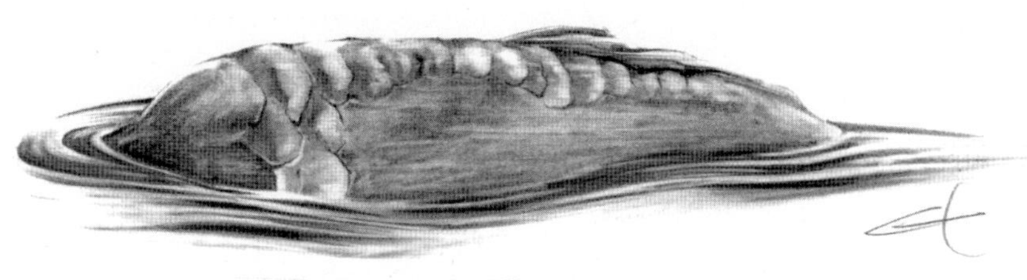

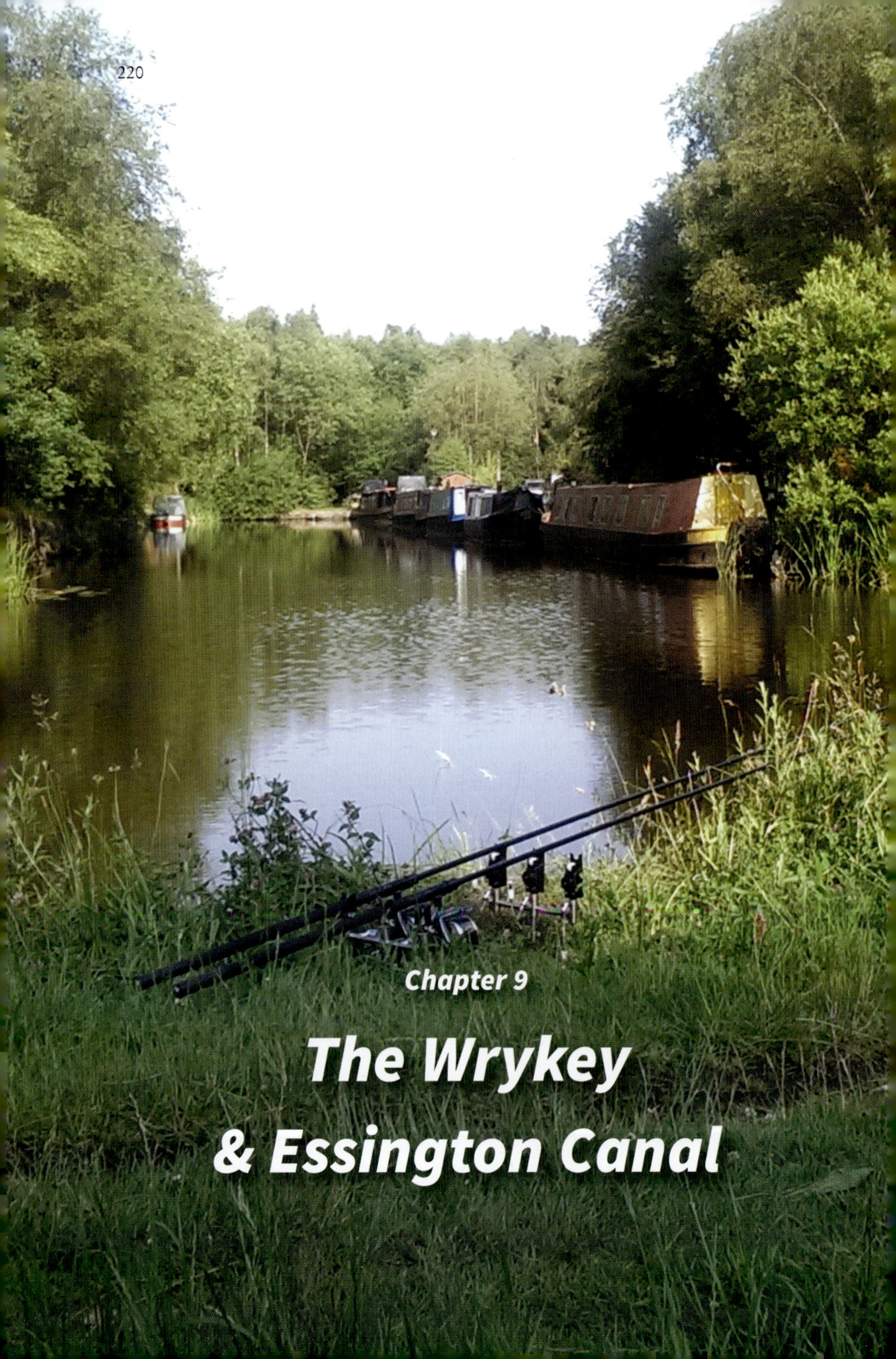

Chapter 9

The Wrykey & Essington Canal

The Wyrley and Essington Canal

By Neil Horton

The Wyrley & Essington canal flows through the heart of the West Midlands, but became of more interest to me as it reached the Pelsall, Brownhills, Walsall Wood & Aldridge regions of this area. Having lived in the village of Clayhanger, Brownhills, all my life, when I began fishing at ten years of age, the 'cut' was where I learned to catch fish on a variety of different methods, & the desire to catch carp was there from an early age. As I progressed through catching roach & perch, then tench & bream, the carp were always going to be targeted by me one day!

When I eventually left school in 1988 (eighteen years ago!) & started work, I started to spend some of my early wage packets on a two rod set-up. It was frighteningly basic! From memory, I had two Sundridge 'Turbo' 1.75lb TC rods, two Sundridge rear drag reels, two 'hi-tone' Optonics, 12lb Maxima main line & I didn't even have a chair, I had to sit on my coat on the floor! My first sessions were totally fruitless, as I really was just finding my feet. I was aware that the other guys, Dave Edwards, Dave Williams, Royston Butwell, Wayne Dunn, Lee Evans, Stu Lines, Micky Eagles & Les Bowd were catching odd fish, & was dying to glean as much information as possible. I hooked my first fish after a night session at Clayhanger. I borrowed my parents camp-bed, & spent the night under my 45" brolly & thin sleeping bag one autumn night. I woke early in the morning because I was freezing, & had zipped the sleeping bag right to the top. Out of the blue, my left hand rod, on a side hooked Richworth 'tutti-fruitti' absolutely flew off, & I couldn't get out of my sleeping bag! When I eventually did get to the rod, it was buried solid in the weed. After a bit of pulling, the rig eventually came back, complete with a straightened out size six Drennan Super Specialist hook! Although I was gutted at losing the fish, I was pleased that at least I knew that I was in the right places to get pick-ups.

Dave Edwards became my closest source of information, & from him I learned most of my carp fishing knowledge. He introduced me to the three inch bolt rig, big leads, line sinkers (back leads), peanuts & pop-ups! I slowly but surely started to notch up a few captures, even though most of these fish were no bigger than low doubles, these early lessons were extremely important. I started to move further afield from Clayhanger (which was easy for me to fish, as I lived about half a mile away), & I paid a lot of attention to an area we referred to as 'Tesco arm', at Brownhills. Here, the 'arm' was a small cut-off from the main canal that was no more than three feet deep, & twenty feet wide & was heavily overgrown. Although most of it was unfishable, because of the trees, it provided us with some great positions to watch the carp closely, so we could study how they behaved.

We quickly realised that all the carp in the canal were nomadic. They would remain in one holding area, until they decided to move - usually down to angling pressure, & they were all resident fish. After five or six years spent carp fishing the canal, all the fish being caught were the same ones over & over again.

There were two known twenties - the biggest of which was a fish known as 'the leather', which seemed to spend most of its time in the arm at 'Tesco bend'. In fact, for all its captures that we were aware of, it was never caught anywhere else! I caught this fish twice, the first time it weighed 22lb 8oz, & the second time I caught it, I didn't have my scales, & it seemed much bigger!

The other was a fish we affectionately named 'Sid'. I was fortunate enough to catch this fish off the surface, mid-summer one year from Catshill junction at 22lb - it's biggest known weight. I also had a fish known as 'the 18' at 20lb 6oz from 'the grove', in Pelsall. These carp were the most noticeable captures from my time on the 'cut', where the average carp was around 12lb in weight, & a good fish would have been perhaps 15lb+.

During the summer of 2008, I made a few visits to an area of the canal in an attempt to stalk a fish known as 'three scale'. I believe this fish was first caught by my mate Dave Edwards some time during the early eighties at around 10lb & I last caught this fish at a weight of 18lb 12oz from Aldridge marina in 2002 & it certainly looked as if it was now over the 20lb mark. Unfortunately, I only had one real chance to hook it on a floating bait due to the blustery conditions on the day. I opted to fish a hastily arranged night session in the area, knowing that there were only two carp in the stretch. The take came in the early hours of the morning & it turned out to be the other fish that I'd spotted – a small common. I found 'three scale' the following day, where it had located to another nearby stretch. During two evening stalking sessions, I caught two fish whilst trying to snare it – both double figure commons! 'Three scale', along with another couple of known fish (one of them being a good upper-double ghostie) are still on my hit list, but unfortunately, my canal fishing is limited to just a handful of opportunistic sessions per season, due to the already limited fishing time I have available being spent targeting bigger venues.

With the weather turning markedly warmer during early May 2009, I was able to sneak a few stalking sessions in, here & there on one or two local stretches. Frustratingly, I'd been unable to locate any decent fish & had only succeeded in catching a couple of small commons – more by accident than design. June subsequently arrived on the back of two weeks of very hot weather & this triggered the carp into spawning activity which lasted for a few days, further increasing my frustration! However, after lots of walking & looking I eventually managed to find & bank my first half decent fish of the summer.

As my evening stalking sessions were limited to no more than just a couple of hours, the need to locate fish & get them feeding as soon as practically possible was extremely important. By keeping a close eye on just a couple of local stretches that I felt would yield the better fish, in most cases I was able to segregate the smaller fish from the decent ones. On one evening, I turned up to find a good breeze blowing along the stretch & I was surprised to find hardly any carp there at all... Out of desperation I followed the floaters that had drifted into the next stretch to find three fish taking the occasional one or two. Luckily the smallest of the group was happily slurping the floaters down on its own, well away from the two better fish – a common & a mirror, both upper doubles. Although the mirror managed to avoid the hookbait on several occasions, the common eventually made its mistake after a very delicate take. At 18lb 10oz, I also realised that this was my biggest canal common to date.

One of the most frustrating things about my evening stalking episodes was the amount of times I would locate fish, get them to feed, then for no reason at all they'd vacate the area completely. I'd also noticed that there were more & more people targeting the canal carp using surface methods. When my friends & I used to fish the canal over twenty years before, we never saw anyone else fishing for them. These days it seems as if everyone is out with a rod, net & half a loaf of bread as soon as the sun comes out!

With the extra pressure on these fish, seeking out quieter stretches where their presence may have been overlooked was now my highest priority.

As early as three weeks prior to the 2010 closed season, on a local stretch of canal I'd been trickling bait into a few likely looking spots on a regular basis – usually on my way home from work in the evenings. A couple of areas in particular were beginning to clear up very nicely, up to the point where it was only a matter of a days to go until I intended to start my canal campaign. Around this time, the main feeder reservoir for the canal system was being drained for repair work & the millions of gallons of water that had been released into the canal added a tinge of unseasonable colour to the water, that suddenly made it difficult to identify whether my spots were being fed on with any regularity. Despite this, I kept the bait going in as I remained confident that fish would still be taking full advantage of the free food source that I was systematically providing for them.

For my first session, the weather conditions were perfect - warm with light rain forecast well into the night. I positioned two hinged stiff rigs onto each of the spots & after backleading both lines out of harms way, I spread thirty baits over the general area. Once the rain arrived, I made myself comfortable under my brolly & got the kettle on. Just as the kettle had boiled, the right-hand Delkim shrieked out & I was on the rod in an instant. Luckily the fish hadn't gone too far & was soon bundled into the net, which turned out to be a feisty common of 18lb 4oz – not a bad start! With a couple of self-take pictures done in the rain, she was soon reunited with her friends & a fresh rig was soon in position with the minimum of fuss. I had several savage liners during the night & I awoke at dawn, quickly packing away before the rain returned. Whilst I stood patiently for a couple of hours, I had several more liners which confirmed that the carp had continued to visit my spots regularly, but something wasn't quite right. When the rain returned around 8:00am I decided enough was enough & I reeled in to go home. I then realised that there was a small 'hump' of weed that my main lines were running over & I was certain that this was the reason for the liners - the fish must have been spooking off the poor line lay as a result. The plan now was to keep the original spots primed & to work on a couple of new areas, but to focus on making sure that in future, the line lay was spot-on.

The following weeks were spent continually priming various spots within the same stretch with a view to getting in a few overnight sessions during the three month period of the normal closed season. Unfortunately, at the time I was in the process of purchasing a new vehicle – a saga that was beginning to drag on & cost me valuable fishing time. Eventually after what seemed like an age, I took delivery of my new 'carp wagon' & I planned to continue the canal campaign in mid April. Whilst planning my next session & keeping the baiting plan in motion, a warm spell in early April presented me with an opportunity to get out onto the canal bank for a spot of floater fishing where I was lucky enough to bank three doubles from two different stretches. Although the best fish was only 14lb, it was nice to get out on the banks in a tee-shirt in the sunshine.

After lots of looking & baiting I settled on priming one particular area, as one or two other carp anglers had begun targeting the same stretch so in order to avoid 'stepping on anyone's toes', I decided to focus my attentions in my new pitch. As far as presentation was concerned, I chose to use balanced bottom-bait presentations, due largely because of the weed-free nature of the two spots. By making sure my lines were backleaded out of the way, I was supremely confident of some action upon my return. Unfortunately, any action was limited to being dragged out of a warm sleeping bag at 1:00am to land a tench of around 3lb & my luck was typified by a carp crashing out right on the spot I'd taken the tench from just minutes earlier while I was trying to remove all the snot & weed from the line & leader! Despite receiving lots of liners throughout the hours of darkness, a take failed to materialise & I headed off home in the early morning for a shower & some breakfast. I returned a couple of hours later with my stalking gear for a day's floater fishing, whereby after walking several miles of canal, I failed to find a single fish!

After spending a couple of evenings searching a few different stretches, I eventually found one stretch where there were evidently a few carp holding up. Although they were difficult to temp largely due to the volume of towpath traffic – dog walkers, joggers & cyclists, I managed to bank two commons in successive evenings – both around mid-doubles.

Following these captures, I spent the following few weeks trying to track down some better fish on various different stretches, but it seemed no matter how hard I looked I simply could not locate many carp above mid-double figures. Eventually, after many hours of searching I managed to find three decent fish – a common & a mirror both around the twenty-pound mark & a slightly smaller common in a quiet area tucked up in a small reedbed. It took a relatively long time to get them taking floaters – I suspect largely due to the very hot temperatures at the time - & at one stage the big mirror appeared right at the edge of the reeds & I flicked my single hookbait just to the left of the spot. Almost immediately another fish appeared & swam straight up to the hoobait & vey gently sipped it in & after a very lively fight I landed the fish – the smallest of the three that turned out to be another common that weighed 15lb exactly.

I spent the following three-week period returning to the stretch where I'd seen the two bigger fish, where they had remained resident during that time. At one point, I'd spent four successive evenings trying to fashion a take from the big mirror & with each opportunity that presented itself, the stubborn creature refused to entertain any notion of sampling my hookbait. Eventually, the ever-increasing mallard, coot & moorhen population almost drove me mad as they would literally 'sweep' the canal, hunting for every last mixer they could find - despite my best attempts to dissuade them. On my last evening of that week & with time running out, I hastily made my way to another stretch where I knew there were a few carp holding up & spent almost three hours drifting floaters on the prevailing breeze. Eventually, with a desperate need for food & with my depleted supply of floaters, I decided enough was enough & I turned to head for my local chip shop. Within seconds, I noticed a deep-bodied swirl appear on the surface in a corner where many of the soggy floaters had drifted. Quick as a flash, I assembled the rod & net & I quietly crept along the bank to get a better look at my potential victim… it looked like a good un'! Very gradually, the dumpy mirror made its way along the margin & I was able to conceal my presence by virtue of the long grass on the edge of the towpath. Having plotted the path of the fish, I flicked the hookbait about six feet in front it & drew it back into position, just two yards from the nearside bank. As it neared the hookbait, the fish turned to head for the middle of the canal & just as I cursed my luck, he inexplicably turned back & headed straight for it. It seemed like an age, but eventually he tentatively slurped it in & I swept the rod back, feeling that satisfying 'thump' as the rod kicked over & the fish made its bid for freedom. After a really feisty scrap, I netted my prize & I knew instantly it was 20lb+. With the photographs taken in the evening sun, the scales revealed a weight of 21lb exactly – my fifth canal twenty. All the trials & tribulations I'd had targeting the mirror on the first stretch were instantly forgotten - happy days!

The following week I returned to the original stretch to see if the big mirror had returned & I couldn't believe my luck when I found it holding-up under a small group of lily pads. Once I'd spent a few minutes drifting floaters into the pads on the breeze, she could resist no longer & eventually took the opportunity for a free feed. After painstakingly trying to get the hookbait into the right position, I eventually hit the right spot & the light breeze slowly pushed the hookbait right in front of the now stationary fish. With the hookbait barely an inch from the nose of the fish, she glared at it for an age before slowly easing forward & sipping at the surface. As the hookbait begun to bob up & down, eventually it disappeared from view & my subsequent strike made her absolutely furious! Holding on for dear life, once I'd made the mistake of allowing her to turn her head she powered off on a simply unstoppable run towards the nearest lily bed & I can quite honestly say, I can't remember ever hooking a carp with that kind of power before in the canal. Trying my damndest to slow the fish down, I eventually 'applied the brakes' just as the fish neared

20lb 6oz.

17lb 8oz.

21lb.

the lily bed, but it was all too much for my 8lb mono & in a split-second it was all over - my first canal loss for a long time. Having landed the 21lb mirror just a week or so earlier, I knew that fish was a good three or four pounds bigger in size...

With the arrival of 16th of June, I returned to Oakwood to see in the beginning of the new season with Ben & Chris & predictably, any activity we'd seen at the lake stopped as soon as the masses descended onto the banks of the lake after three months of relative peace. I continued my floater fishing excursions on the canal, whilst I made plans to get back to Oakwood in last weeks of June & managed to bank three fish in three sessions during one week - a small scaley mirror & two upper-double commons. Although I was continuing to bank a few fish & their average size was improving, the really big fish were still proving difficult to locate. On one occasion, I found a good-sized mirror, but it was continually flanked by a pack of four smaller fish, so trying to single that one fish out was a difficult task. I eventually managed to get a take from it at close range, only to bump the hook out on the strike! Just when I thought I'd blown any opportunity of catching, I found an average-sized common feeding at close range which when hooked, the fight proved to be most bizarre... As the fish charged up & down the margins in its bid for freedom, it was being followed side-by-side by a smaller mirror. When the common was ready to net, the mirror dived in there with him & when I lifted it & realised what had happened, all hell broke loose as the mirror furiously tried to swim through the mesh! I had to be really careful to make sure that the mirror could swim out without risking letting the hooked common out too- madness!

My subsequent return to the canal was after a period of very hot weather in mid-June where the air temperature had dropped markedly & I was sure that the carp had finished spawning, so I made my way along the canal looking at the usual stretches, but with no luck. Eventually I managed to locate a group of three small commons & after getting them competing for floaters, I realised that indeed there were quite a few fish resident & I managed to identify a good upper-double figure mirror. After a couple of unsuccessful attempts at trying to single out the biggest mirror, I suddenly became aware of a big white shape below the group of feeding fish that slowly came up to the surface revealing the one fish that I'd been searching for the last three or four years - the big twenty pound plus ghost carp that I'd heard countless rumours about, but had never actually seen in the flesh before. Here it was, in front of me & wolfing down floaters like he didn't have a care in the world! Hurriedly, I glued on a new floater & by this time my hands were shaking & the ghostie was mopping up every floater in its path. When I was ready to cast out, the ghostie disappeared & every now & again he would reappear from the far bank, eat two or three floaters, then drift back out of sight again. It was mad to be standing there, watching a group of six or seven carp troughing down floaters in front of me - with one or two good upper doubles there too & yet I was totally focussed on hooking the ghostie. The feeding pattern of the fish was the same every time, so I knew that each time it appeared, I would have to make sure that the hookbait was placed perfectly, as I was probably only going to get one window of opportunity. On several occasions I tried to position the hookbait, but each time he wasn't interested - almost as if he'd already identified which three floaters he was going to eat on each showing. On a number of occasions, I even had to drag the hookbait away from the mouth of a feeding fish so that I didn't spook the biggun! With the light fading quickly, he again reappeared & I tried to plot its path again once more. Having taken two floaters, he turned & headed back towards his hidey-hole & I flicked the hookbait out into his return route. Up he came with purpose & sucked it in with gusto & I struck... sending the hookbait whizzing past me into the bush behind me & with that my chance was gone. I did hook & land a solitary token low-double mirror as compensation, but I was still sick about failing to take the golden opportunity that I had been presented with.

I managed to get back to the spot where I'd seen the big ghostie just two days later where amazingly, it appeared almost immediately once I'd begun introducing floaters. Just as I thought my luck was in, I managed to hook it on my very first cast, but as it headed off towards the far side, the 8lb mainline disintegrated under the pressure & I reasoned that my one opportunity had gone. To my surprise, an hour or so later he reappeared taking floaters again, albeit very cautiously. On three separate occasions he came up to the hookbait for a closer inspection only to reject it at the very last moment until on the fourth attempt he accepted it as a genuine freebie & just I had done the first time round, I struck the hookbait straight back out of its mouth! As is generally the case for me, whether it's because I report freely though this website or not I'm not sure, but the area that I'd been targeting the big ghostie all of a sudden became a hive of activity & over the following few days, the area received a lot of attention from other anglers... Since that time, I'd not seen or indeed even heard of the ghostie being hooked or landed so I've not given up all hope yet. Whilst trying to find the fish, I'd got a few fish going quite well on floaters, however these were generally only very small & my frustration has been compounded further by hooking & landing one or two of them.

Just when I was questioning (& ultimately dismissing) all the 'thirty rumours' that I continuously keep hearing about the Wyrley & Essington canal in this area, I was contacted by a local carp angler to tell me of his capture of a proper canal 'chunk' - a mirror in excess of 31lb. As it happens, this fish came from a stretch of local canal that I was fortunate to hold a ticket for last season. Having visited the stretch on a couple of occasions, I got talking to a couple of lads that had also been targeting the same area with some impressive results. One of the lads even showed me a couple of pictures of the 'thirty' at lower weights, which just goes to show that this particular fish has continued to grown-on. So as a result of the ever-increasing pressure on the other stretches of canal that I've been fishing, I've decided to move away from my normal haunts & focus my efforts here. Certainly with this unique capture, I've renewed my ticket & my hopes of banking a big-canal fish have taken on new importance it's just a matter of finding them.

After a lot of thought, I decided to relocate to another stretch of canal for a short time, mainly because my confidence needed a bit of a lift. I needed to put an effective rig & good quality bait in front of feeding fish to reaffirm their effectiveness. After a couple of visits to an area where I knew for a fact that they were resident, I had managed to land one bream & lose a small carp by fishing to a marginal reed bed. Once I gave it a bit of thought, I opted to revert back to fishing simple blowback style arrangements with five inch coated hooklinks & a single bottom bait. A short leadcore leader & a doctored lead-clip that allowed the 2.5oz lead to discharge straight away completed the simple, no-nonsense setup.On my third session, I positioned both rigs tight to the far bank reeds & loosely scattered six or seven b aits between them & despite no real signs that carp were present, I gave it about two hours until I decided I'd had enough & rather foolishly, went to have a look at the marginal reed bed that I would normally have fished to, no more than twenty yards away. Suddenly, the right hand Neville one-noted & I ran back to the rods as fast as I could & once I'd made contact with the fish, I was aware that it had gone crashing through the reeds at some speed! After giving it lots of stick, the fish begrudgingly started to work its way back to the fringe of the reed bed when the hook pulled, typifying my recent luck. On closer inspection, it transpired that the size six Stiff-Rigger had opened out quite severely - worse than I'd ever seen before & thinking about the episode has led me to believe that considering the situation I was fishing in, that perhaps it was a little foolish of me to be so 'under-gunned' - a lesson well learned! I've since been doing some strength tests on several different hook patterns & to be honest, to suggest the results have been eye-opening would be an understatement. Even some popular patterns that have an excellent reputation when it comes to strength, I've proven to be nothing short of useless when put under extreme pressure. At least I'd managed to prove that the rig & importantly, the bait was working fine. Bait-wise, I'd chosen to go back to using a popular bait that I have absolute faith in. The reason for this was because I couldn't afford to purchase bait from my preferred supplier, FIVE STAR in bulk due to my precarious financial situation. I needed to be able to purchase smaller quantities of a shelf-life bait at a lower cost locally, so by returning back to my old faithful bait, my confidence was on a high. Many would probably question why I selected a shelf-life bait; the reason being painfully simple - I needed to carry a reasonable quantity of bait with me on my Oakwood sessions, but didn't want to keep re-freezing what bait I didn't use as I simply couldn't afford to waste it. With confidence returning, I was sure my luck would change soon - it was time to return to the spot where the bigguns lived & put the prebaiting plan back into the motion again.

I managed a mere handful of sessions since the end of August - each no more than two hours in duration, banking a mid-double mirror & common respectively. Following a sneaky overnighter in the first week of November, I lost a fish in the small hours of the morning & I woke to find that the hinged stiff-link on the other rod had tangled – the first time I'd ever had this happen. To compound matters, within minutes of repositioning both rigs & receiving a series of liners, a group of around twenty anglers arrived to fish an impromptu match... I just couldn't believe my luck. Feeling very disgruntled, I made my way back to the car but stopped when I noticed some movement on the edge of a decaying reedbed. Clearly carp were in the area so I quickly 'underarmed' a single hookbait to the spot where the carp had shown & just as the activity started to become more significant, my time was up & I had to leave. Realising that if I'd spotted those fish earlier, I would have had a decent chance of nicking a bite, so I returned early the following morning hoping to capitalise on my find. I got to the bankside at around 7:00am & I decided to use one rod only as I felt that two rods in the area would have been counterproductive. With the aid of my baiting pole, I quietly delivered the rig (a single 18mm bottom-bait on three-inch braided hooklink & a three ounce inline flat pear lead mounted drop-off style & a handful of finely crumbed baits in a tiny, solid PVA bag) to the front edge of the reeds. Within ten minutes I spotted subtle signs that signalled carp were still in the area & that my 'trap setting' had obviously gone unnoticed. I watched the water intensely for an hour & I became increasingly concerned that most of the activity was to the right side of the reedbed, where it was apparent that they used this side as a route to enter in & out of it. With time running out, I decided to reposition the rig. I quickly tied up another PVA bag & tried to get the small food package as close to the 'entrance' as I could. Again, it looked as though I'd got away with it until the first narrow boat of the day came ploughing through the stretch around five minutes later, forcing me to reposition the rig again – it was almost farcical such was my bad luck. Once the boat had continued on its way I decided against using the pole to get the rig back out as it was probably half a metre short of where I needed the rig to be, so I opted to just foam up the hook & swing the rig out. The first cast was not quite far enough, but the second cast went 'bang on the money' & I flicked a couple of broken baits out into the small gap in the reeds. Once the backlead was in place, I had barely just snapped the lid back on the bucket when I heard the reel clutch click a couple of times & looked up to see the rod tip hooped round to the right. Quickly I heaved the fish clear of the reedbed & after a decent fight, I had a gorgeous little mid-double mirror nestling in the folds of my landing net. At 15lb 12oz, I was pleased with my mornings work & after all my recent bad luck, I hoped that things would finally begin to improve a little going into winter. Once I'd returned home, I got to work playing around with various old spare sections of poles & managed to extend the length of the baiting pole by another two metres – hopefully, this would be my ultimate weapon for getting the most out of the stretch of canal I'd planned to concentrate on for the remainder of the season.

The harsh conditions of the following weeks that led into winter consigned my fishing tackle to the confines of my house for a seven week period from the end of November - perhaps the longest single period of time where I've not been able to wet a line in recent memory. However, during early February I resumed fishing on the canal after my frustration with Oakwood reached a peak & I opted to spend the remaining few weeks of the traditional season back on the stretch that I'd fished last time out. Clearly the fish were much less active since the severity of the cold conditions & it had clearly made a massive impact on fish movements. This made pin-pointing the areas where the carp were holding up, much more difficult to identify & I was certain that they were lying tight under the tree-lined far margin where it was almost impossible to position a rig effectively. I tried a few different areas where I felt there was a good chance of them turning up, but all to no avail. I did manage to find a couple of fish on one occasion, but they simply refused to feed despite passing freely over my baited spots & after a lot of thought & perhaps through almost total desperation, I begun to pre-bait a spot where my gut-feeling told me they just had to be. The spot in question was in three feet of water & between two overhanging trees where the bottom was silty & had a few twigs & dead leaves scattered about it. As good presentation & line lay was critical, I spent one evening with a spod rod & small castable rake clearing the area of twigs & leaves until I was happy that I could begin introducing bait on a regular basis. I made a conscious decision to revert back to using my all-time favorite rig & one that I had the utmost confidence in – the awesome hinged stiff-link pop-up. By employing this set-up, I could position the rig tight to the branches of the tree with an underarm cast & by using a small piece of PVA foam on the hook, I could guarantee my traps would be setup as perfectly as I could get them.

With the impending arrival of the normal closed season, I had one more opportunity to fish the stretch that I'd been targeting since the end of August 2010, but after a bit of thought I reluctantly decided to move away from that stretch to begin my campaign on a different stretch for the next three months. After identifying an area where I believed the carp could be holding-up, I spent five days prior to my session priming two separate areas – stopping off to introduce a small amount of boilies & tigers on my way home from work each evening. Upon inspecting the spots each day, the bait was being cleared from the spots & one spot in particular begun to 'glow' as the clay-lined canal bed was being systematically revealed after bait had been applied to it. When I arrived for my first session, I set up in the area I was most confident in, but checked the clay spot on my way to my other area - again, the bottom had been completely cleaned off. In my usual spot, the bottom was still littered with areas of patchy weed & with this in mind, I opted to fish chod rigs on both rods with a scattering of approximately twenty baits & a few complimentary grains of corn in the hope of getting any passing fish to investigate. Just before dark, I decided to scatter a handful of corn onto the 'clay spot' & I planned to keep an eye on it during the night. At 7:30pm I had two savage liners on the right-hand rod, followed by another on the left-hand rod & I put this down to fishing semi-tight lines that I wasn't able keep tight to the canal bed because of the random patches of weed. After a few minutes, I decided to slacken the lines off completely, feeding a couple of feet of line off both spools, hoping that this would prevent any feeding fish from spooking off the baited area. At

10:30pm I decided to go & check the clay spot. I crept up to area & shone the sharp beam of the head torch onto the spot... All I could make out was a cloud of silt lingering in mid-water & I could just about make out the tail of a carp in the middle of it. Suddenly, the fish straightened up & bolted from the area & I realised that this was an area that I needed to prime regularly. Once I'd returned back to the warmth of my sleeping bag, the next thing I remember was waking to a short, sharp succession of bleeps at 1:30am from the right-hand Neville & I soon had my boots on & doing battle with what I first thought was a tench, that actually turned out to be a long & scaley mid-double mirror – my first carp of 2011. After setting up a new rig, I got it back into position & climbed back into the bag. I was awake at the crack of dawn to do some quick self-takes & I quickly departed as I was due to attend the ECHO AGM in Aldershot later that day, stopping off to introduce some more bait onto the clay spot before loading up the car.

Although I managed to spend a couple of evening sessions fishing the 'clay spot', I could never really stay late enough into the night to reap the benefits as it was definitely being fed on during the small hours of the morning. It also seemed as if another couple of anglers had cottoned onto what I had been up to & they subsequently took advantage of my hard work. In all fairness, they may or may not have realised that I had been prepping the spot for some time as it wasn't particularly difficult to locate, any carp angler worth his salt would have realised that once my little spot begun to 'glow' white as it was repeatedly being polished by feeding fish, that they would have to get on it, so whilst I wasn't particularly happy with the situation, I couldn't really blame them. The effect of this, along with the ever-improving weather conditions, I decided to change tact & revert to stalking any future captures & with the spring sun making its first proper appearance during the third week of March, I managed to bank my first surface-caught fish of the year which must be a record for me as I can't remember the last time I managed to get fish taking floaters in March! This was even more surprising as there had been a sharp frost only the night before... I'd spent a few weeks examining the usual haunts looking for fish & most of them were almost devoid of any carp & in recent years, I have

19lb 4oz.

20lb.

21lb 8oz.

come to realise that this is normally due to an increase in water temperature that prepares them for spawning activity & invariably, the vast majority of these fish can be found in one single area. After a little thought & more than a few hours searching I found them. Evidently there were a large number of fish present in the stretch, but frustratingly, it became almost impossible to identify the larger residents due to the amount of fish that were present & the low-light conditions. On my first stalking session, I managed just one take which I missed completely, but I was fortunate to conjure a return three days later for an inopportune session... I arrived very late one Sunday evening with barely an hour or so of light & poor conditions for floater fishing – a strong & cold north-easterly wind. I had little more than a couple of handfuls of floaters after I had completely forgotten to put some more in my bag, but I figured it was still worth spending what little time I had available having a quick look as I've learned over the years that you never quite know what opportunities the unpredictable canal fish might provide. I drifted a few floaters along the more sheltered areas of the stretch, where the carp had shown a few days previously, but there was no interest. Reluctantly, I decided to check out the extreme windward end of the area before I made my way home. After around ten minutes I decided enough was enough & just as I was about to leave I spotted a subtle flat-spot appear in the ripples around ten yards out... I pulted out a few more floaters in the general area & sure enough just a few moments later, a big set of white lips pierced through the surface ripple. As quick as my legs could carry me, I raced further along the bank where I could hopefully get a better view of the fish & I could just about make out a light-coloured fish moving about slowly beneath the surface. I cast out my free-lined hookbait as best as I could, but the wind was making it impossible to reach the required range & with time running out fast & with the light disappearing, I noticed a second fish that had joined in & was taking a few floaters that had drifted into the margins a few yards further along the bank. Knowing that this was my best chance of a take as I could just flick the hookbait along the edge of the marginal reed bed, I took up my position, crouched behind the reed stems. For a few minutes the activity had all but stopped & I was starting to curse my mistake of not bringing enough floaters when there was a large swirl just inches from the reeds to my left. Within seconds I cast the hookbait six feet out, then slowly dragged it back into position around two feet from the edge of the reeds. No more than thirty seconds later the water started to shift below the hookbait & out came those unmistakable lips as the fish slurped in my hookbait & as soon as I struck it surged off on a powerful run that forced me to pay off line at a fast rate. As the fight progressed, the fish made several unstoppable runs that left me in no doubt that I was going to lose it, but as it began to tire, I knew it was a good 'un & it was looking promising that I might just bank the unseen fish. As I shifted the landing net into position, with steady pressure the fish bobbed up on the surface & I inched her slowly over the net cord. When I lifted her out of the water & lay her down in the soft grass I knew straight away it was the 'big ghostie' – the fish I'd heard about on so many occasions & I'd been unlucky enough to waste a couple of good chances to bank her the season before. My mind raced as to how big she was & with the light virtually disappearing, I rattled off a succession of self-take pictures where she behaved implicitly. With the scales revealing a weight of 25lb exactly, the capture was of major significance to my fishing for a number of reasons: firstly it was a new canal personal best & after over twenty years of fishing these stretches, I'd never seen a fish of this size in the canal before, secondly it was both my personal best common & ghost carp & thirdly, it left me free to concentrate my canal fishing solely on just one area where the other canal fish of my desire resides – a gorgeous old scaley warrior that last visited the bank at over 31lb...

I managed to make another two visits to the same stretch within the following week, the first of these was a midweek evening visit whilst the weather had remained warm & sunny throughout the day, but the evening temperatures had dropped rapidly due to the stiff north eastern breeze – hardly the best conditions for surface fishing. I spent around thirty minutes trying to locate some fish & I eventually found a small group in an area by an old overflow & I was able to get a take from a good common almost straight away that saw me strike the hookbait clean from its mouth. Luckily, the fish didn't seem too spooked, but I got the distinct feeling that it had made them a little bit more 'edgy'. Once I'd spent the remaining hour or so chasing fish up & down the stretch I did fashion another take, but with the same end result. Two days later I arrived again to find four or five fish lying in a sparse area of weed, just inches from the surface. After catapulting a handful of floaters upwind of the group of fish, they soon become more active & they begun to feed on them with confidence. One of these fish appeared to be a decent twenty pound plus common that had followed the floaters out of the swim on the prevailing wind. Once the floaters had disappeared, they returned looking for more & I flicked my single hookbait into the path of the common that took it readily at the first attempt. Foolishly, I then realised that I hadn't set up a landing net, so once I figured that the fish had tired enough, I engaged the baitrunner on the reel, dropped the rod into the reeds & put the net together as quick as I possibly could. I assembled the net & threw it into the water & picked up the rod expecting the fish to have taken lots of line to find that it was just sulking in the weed in front of the swim. Once I managed to free it, it came up to the surface & straight into the waiting net. Due to the protracted fight, my initial concern was that it might have been due to spawning preparation, so I inspected the fish thoroughly & fortunately everything was in good order. The one thing that really struck me about it was that it had a huge floppy tail that looked as if it belonged to a fish twice its size! The fish did seem excessively stressed on the bank, so I weighed the fish & took a few self-takes as fast as I could – I wanted to get this fish back as quickly as possible. At 21lb 8oz, it was a great result & further proof that the canal fish have really grown-on within the last few years. It seems strange now that only ten years or so ago, there were only two known twenties in the canal around this area – now there are significantly more.

By the end of May, many of the fish I'd found held up in one particular area of the canal had eventually dispersed back into the system, yet their appearance in the normal areas that I would expect to find them was proving to be very slow. However, I did manage to hook & ultimately lose one of the better fish that I'd seen at the time – a stunning fully-scaled, mid-twenty mirror that proved to be more than a match for my relatively light stalking tackle after hooking it in the margins of a snaggy swim once

I'd spent hours coaxing it to take a few floaters. For a sustained period of around three weeks, the windy conditions made location extremely difficult & I subsequently found it very hard to find even a single fish. Eventually, as the conditions began to improve, I managed to bank a succession of mid-to-upper doubles from a couple of stretches that were extremely welcome visitors to my landing net, but I couldn't help thinking how I blew my chances of catching some really good fish whilst they were all held-up in that one single area.

As is usual, it seemed as if my actions weren't going unnoticed as a few anglers were beginning to appear in the areas that I'd been fishing, so with the onset of a new season I plan to resume my evening stalking sessions on another stretch in an attempt to find my one remaining target fish... I know that I've got my work cut out trying to locate it & I know there's going to be a few more anglers looking for the same fish this year so I'll just have to be patient & make sure I'm fishing at 100% whenever I'm on the bank.

In a strange twist of fate, my target fish that had been conspicuous by its absence had evolved sufficiently to grow legs & it eventually turned up at another lake around the Lichfield area... At the time, I was informed by a friend who was also notified by a lad who had caught the same fish on three separate occasions. Whilst I was mortified by the theft of one of the largest carp that there had ever been in this canal, I was left to question the merits of such a disgraceful act. After all, the fish in question had almost certainly spent its entire life in the canal & the perpetrators of the crime obviously never cared about this creatures welfare & perhaps more importantly, the welfare of the stock of the small pool it was moved to. After all, there are no disease controls for the canal fish & there's nothing to suggest that the fish that was stolen isn't carrying any viruses (& I know for a FACT that this fish wasn't the only one that was moved illegally...). What is also most frustrating is that this fish will almost certainly never fulfill its true potential in its new home - a small hole-in-the-ground of less than acre in size, where it is now under serious competition for food, whereas in the canal, it had little competition for sustainable food sources. It is a real shame & certainly isn't the first fish to be stolen from the canal

& evidently wont be the last, with many of our Eastern European counterparts also seeking these harmless creatures for their dinner table. The situation is now getting very serious & exactly how much this upsets the canals eco-system is anyone's guess, but for sure these are sad times for the Wyrley & Essington canal & its days as a thriving environment for these creatures are without doubt, numbered. Since the news has broken, various authorities have been notified including ECHO, British Waterways & fishery officers of the controlling club from the stretch of canal from where the fish was taken from. Hopefully, they will be able to prevent these 'anglers' from from doing any more damage & better still, bring them to some sort of justice... I now know of three local lakes that hold a number of ex-canal fish. I also know some of the areas where they are being stolen from.

With this whole sorry episode, my plans have been somewhat thrown into disarray once more. Where I'd planned to focus much of my efforts on the stretch of canal where the big mirror was removed from, now it all seems pretty pointless & I'll have to seriously rethink my plans for the forthcoming winter period. Targeting specific fish is difficult enough without the added fear that someone might beat you to it & move it to another small 'puddle' somewhere else... To my mind, any fish theft (regardless of species) seems to add fire the anti-angling campaigns, making our sport more difficult to justify. Herein is the reason I joined ECHO, to help prevent the selfish acts of others & to protect the fish we care about. Unfortunately, where there is a market for it, some will always be willing to take advantage of such a situation.

As the daytime temperatures begun to decline from the beginning of September, any stalking opportunities were suddenly at a premium. Even the occasional warm spell that presented a chance to get the canal fish feeding within the surface layers seemed to be just not quite warm enough. In the last week of September & during an enforced break from fishing at Oakwood, I was presented with an opportunity to fit two overnight sessions in successive weeks. As luck would have it, I remembered that there was one particular spot in an area of canal that I'd located the previous year with a lead rod, that for one reason or another I neglected to fish, but kept it in mind. The spot in question was just in front of an occasionally moored boat where a small bush overhung the water tight to the far bank. The bottom here was certainly much firmer & was consistently weed-free – almost certainly a regular feeding spot for the canal fish. I managed to get to the bankside about half an hour before dark & quickly positioned two hinged stiff-linked pop-up rigs to the far bank, with one directly on the spot & another slightly to the left of it. I liberally spread about thirty baits around the general area, but tight to the bank – I didn't want all my baits tightly grouped in one area, I wanted any fish in the vicinity to work their way along the far margin looking for individual baits & I placed extra emphasis on making sure that no baits landed short of the rig to ensure that any fish that visited the area wouldn't be feeding over my main lines. With the traps set just into dark, I set about erecting the Ultralite as quietly as possible, pushing the pegs silently into the soft ground with my boots & lifting the bedchair into position without making a sound to ensure my presence was not given away, when literally as the rigs had been in place for no longer than fifteen minutes, the right-hand Neville signalled a fast take. At first it seemed as if the fish was still in the area where it had initially been hooked, but after a couple of powerful lunges, everything was locked-up solid. With the headtorch on, I still couldn't make out where the unseen snag was & I applied pressure from all sorts of different angles in order to get the fish moving. For all the pulling I could muster, I resorted to slackening off the line & putting the rod back on the rests & watching the line closely to see if the fish would move out of the snag of its own accord. Over the next half an hour, the line would periodically pull up tight & I would resume applying extra pressure to the fish, but it simply refused to budge. After weighing up all my options, I eventually opted to pull for a break & fortunately, the rig came back complete with the hook - at least I knew that the fish was not tethered to the snag in any way. With a new rig tied up, I positioned it slightly further away from the offending snag & after a short visit from a friend, I got my head down for the night. At some time around 2:00am I landed a small mirror on the same rod that was around 10lb which was quickly unhooked & returned & I packed away at first light & made my way home. The next week I was back in the same swim, fishing the same area & this session produced another take from the spot at around 10:00pm that turned out to be a small common of around 2lb! This was probably the smallest carp I'd ever caught from the canal & despite its small size; it certainly bodes well for the canals future.

With my subsequent resumption of my Oakwood campaign during mid-October producing two carp – including a new personal best mirror of 34lb, my original intention of relocating to the canal at the end of the year has now been put on-hold. Initially, I'd fully anticipated focussing on the canal for the winter, purely to maintain a degree of action through the colder months, but having learned some extremely important lessons at Oakwood, it seemed almost ludicrous to move off there whilst I now considered these fish to be 'catchable'. This is not to say that I don't intend to fish the canal at all – there will be times when it just won't be practical to fish Oakwood at certain times & these will be the ideal opportunities to drop in on the canal to try & lure one or two of the better fish that I'm certain still exist in the system...

My attention switched back to the canal during the early part of April 2012, following the closure of Oakwood just a month earlier. Unfortunately, as the weather was painfully slow to improve, I struggled to locate a single fish during the first few weeks. I visited all of their usual haunts & even ventured to areas where I didn't expect them to be, but they were unusually conspicuous by their absence.

During the second week of May, I decided to take a look at a stretch where in previous years I have found numbers of carp holding up when the air temperatures begin to improve during the late spring / early summer. After drifting floaters into all of the usual spots, it was evident that there were either no fish in the area, or they were simply unwilling to feed upon the surface. After around an hour, I'd eventually I'd had enough & headed back home, walking along another stretch which is normally devoid of any carp at all, when I caught a sudden glimpse of a dark fish moving slowly alongside the far bank reedbed. Within seconds, I had pulted a handful of floaters a few yards in front of its intended course & watched events unfold closely. At first he swam straight past them, but just a moment later he doubled-back & very tentatively sucked one in. That was all the encouragement I needed & I quickly set up a rod & landing net whilst keeping a close eye on the whereabouts of the fish. The fish travelled a few yards further to a slightly wider area of the canal that was a little more sheltered from the breeze & began to pick off the occasional floater, until it drifted underneath a small raft of dead reeds. A few minutes later it reappeared with another fish that was significantly larger & I watched them drift along the far margin picking off any floater that was close to the reed stems. All of a sudden the smaller fish picked up speed & was now around two meters in front of the biggun'. I instantly knew this was my opportunity & I flicked my hookbait across, almost landing on the head of the small mirror & no more than an inch off the reeds – I couldn't have placed it by hand in a more perfect position! I watched the bigger mirror cruise slowly along the edge of the reeds, shifting its course ever-so-slightly & moving away from my hookbait. Just as I thought my chance had gone, it stopped dead, shifted its head to the right & slowly rose to the surface & sipped in my hookbait, barely making a ripple as it

25lb – Ghostie.

did so. For a split-second, I was unsure whether it had actually taken the hookbait & my resulting strike saw the surface erupt as it headed for the dense reedbed. Luckily, I got the fish under control relatively quickly & I soon had it angrily charging up & down the middle of the canal in its bid for freedom. After around five minutes I had it safely in the bottom of the net & I was sure it was a twenty… The weighing procedure was a formality – 22lb exactly.

As I tidied my kit away after taking a few pictures, I noticed that the odd floater was still being taken, so I quickly set up a new hookbait & scanned the area in an attempt to locate the culprit & soon found the dark fish that I'd seen originally which appeared to be an upper-double. It took me around half an hour until it started to take floaters with any purpose & I was aware that there were also two other smaller fish there too. I watched the dark fish drift slowly into a group of reeds & I cast my hookbait to the other side of it, expecting the fish to reappear, when out-of-the-blue, I saw a swirl & the hoobait was gone. A swift strike revealed it was one of the two smaller fish & after a brief fight it was netted, un-hooked & released without too much fuss. Unfortunately, all this commotion proved too much for the dark mirror & despite hanging around for another hour or so, it had clearly vacated the stretch & moved to pastures new...

Chapter 10

The Grand Union Canal

Grand Carping

By Dan Cleary

My love of fishing on canals started at a young age. I was fortunate that I grew up a short cycle ride away from the Grand Union Canal. I loved going to the canal after school or at weekends back then, even before I even owned any fishing tackle, watching the perch and roach swim by under bushes or the bridges, darting off as I spooked them in my haste to try and get a closer look. Eventually I saved up enough to buy some tackle, and the first place I wet a line was on the canal. Some 25 or so years later, and I've fished many waters since then, even rivers and canals in France, Belgium and Holland. I still have the odd night on the Grand Union, although nowhere near as often as I used too.

My fondest memories fishing have been with friends on the canal, getting up to all sorts of antics and catching a few along the way as well. Some of those stories were written and printed here in BC back in the 90s or early noughties. One of my favourite captures was back in October 1992. I was fishing during a very wet and windy night with inadequate tackle to keep me sheltered from the weather, as it was back then, with my friend and his dad. Trying in vain to shelter under my friend's brolly, with the cover flapping all over the place, and us both half wet half dry, when one of the alarms shrieks out early that night. I rushed out slipping and sliding on the wet grass to finally grab hold of the offending rod in the pouring rain, which was nearly horizontal in the howling wind, while I became attached to some angry beast swimming at 100 miles an hour.

Eventually, it took us under a dual carriageway bridge and out of the rain for a minute or two, before it headed back towards the area to where I originally hooked it and back out into the wind and rain. I went with it, and eventually this monstrous grey lump swirled on the surface and dived down again. My heart was in my mouth at this point, and I just held on for dear life. I'd never seen anything as big before. Finally my friend's dad scooped the hulking grey fish into the net and gave me a big pat on the back. "That's a big one, that is, Dan." I nearly collapsed on the floor at that moment. The fish weighed 28lb 4oz, a big carp then for a UK canal, and some 6 or 7lb bigger than I'd caught or had seen on the bank before. I was soaked to the bone holding her up for the camera, and I didn't care one single bit.

There were four or five of us who fished the canal quite regularly back then, and I am still friends with a couple of them today. A couple of us had fished some local club waters, but they were getting busy, and the fish went to the low 20lb mark, while we knew the canal had produced the odd bigger fish, but only a few in the area knew back then. It was a steep learning curve for me, and add to that getting used to everything that came along the towpaths and the boats thrown in for good measure. My first season, if you call it that, June to October in 1991, was a complete blank except for one double off the surface!

It was not until the following year 1992 that I got to grips with the canal fully and truly fell in the love with the place, with the 28lb already mentioned helping to cement that feeling. The odd fish had a nickname, but most did not, and over the next couple of seasons, some of the fish acquired names by me and my mates to tell them apart, and to try to get an idea on the numbers in this particular stretch on the Grand Union Canal, which stretches around 12-13 miles between the two locks. We found over time some fish were rather residential and didn't venture far, while others, possibly the older carp, were more nomadic and travelled further afield, some covering the whole 13-mile stretch. Rightly or wrongly it was during this time that I learnt, by pooling our knowledge together instead of being a bunch of secret squirrels, that we all learnt something from each other, be it rigs, baits, fish movement, capture times and so on, and so we all shared in the results and learned about the fish a lot quicker than we could ever do on our own. I remember many a night at mine or my friend's house concocting the next winning bait, some good, some not so good. It may have at the time affected our fishing by publishing our results, but we learnt so much by being open and honest about everything with each other. I think that is why I always will be like that. I know some people don't like it, but I don't see how we can advance as a group of carp anglers by hording everything to ourselves, so preaching over with and back to the canal fishing!

I caught many carp over the next couple of seasons, until I become a father in 1994 and hung my rods up for a few years. Most of them thought I had given up and sold my gear, but I had no intention of that, god forbid! Remember these were the days before mobile phones, just.

One of the more significant captures, although it wouldn't have been so at the time, was a 19lb mirror that we nicknamed Cluster. I'd caught it with a couple of others from an entrance to a marina back in the summer of 1993, which was a good season for me on the canal. My friend then caught the same fish in 1997 at 27lbs a mile north of the marina. Then roll on a few years, and in 2007 my partner and I got our first and current house together. This put us me a stone's throw from the canal (I have no idea how that happened!), our neighbour's garden being the only thing between us and the canal's towpath. The hedgerow at the bottom of his garden became

28lb 4oz, October 1992.

Early days on the canal.

29lb 12oz.

my second home for a couple of seasons. I'd fished the area couple of times in the past while on my travels trying to find different and better spots, catching a couple of upper doubles from this section, so I knew they did frequent this area from time to time. I'd also witnessed a group of fish one summer spawning here, although I'm not entirely sure why they did that particular summer, as they usually do their spawning in a marina amongst the weed beds and away from boat traffic.

So I spent a little campaign of midweek overnighters at the bottom of my neighbour's garden, regularly baiting up a couple of times a week, and using any leftovers from my weekend fishing on the Wraysbury lakes in the heart of the Colne Valley. I was hoping to have some different fish I'd not caught but had photos or had seen photos of, one being a 36lb mirror my friend had caught, and I'd also seen on the bank a few years before at 29lbs. The baiting up was working, and I was having doubles and low twenties on a regular basis. It all culminated in the summer of 2007 when trotting down the alley way to the canal with the gear on my back for my regular 12-hour 7pm to 7am overnighter. It looked really good to me, it had been a sticky, hot June day, but had turned overcast during early evening with a nice southerly breeze blowing from my left along the canal, and with rain forecast to come in soon.

I placed both rods in my now usual spots on either side of the canal with a small scattering of boilies and hemp. I decided on this night to change my rigs and fish helicopter style. I'm not really sure why; I just fancied a change of tack. I got the rigs on their spots, and then got my bedchair and brolly up not long before the rain arrived. You don't always see fish on the canals these days, but I did that night. I could also make out some bubbling on the far margin rod. I got in the sleeping bag and pulled it over my head to protect me from the mozzies, but left it unzipped, as it was still fairly hot, and I got myself sheltered from the wind and rain. The rain must have stopped because I was woken around 1am to the far margin rod signalling a slow take.

I slipped and nearly landed on my rods, but managed to get back on my feet and grab the rod and disengage the baitrunner. The fish nearly pulled the rod out of my hands, such was the power of its initial run. I loosened the clutch, as I didn't want to pull the hook. The fish was taking line slowly but steadily, and every time I tried to apply pressure and cup the spool, the fish would kick and take more line. This happened a couple of times. The fish was some way down to my left and had gone through some weed, as I could feel that the angle of the line was not right and that grating feeling you get with weed on the line. I had no choice but to try and follow the fish by walking along the towpath to try to dislodge the weedbed. I got to the offending weedbed 40 or so yards down the towpath, and after a couple of attempts the line pinged free, and I was in direct contact with the fish again.

The fish felt big and heavy as well, staying on the bottom and plodding along as big carp do. It then turned, changed direction on me, and started another run to my right. This posed some danger, and it was heading back to the reed bed I had originally hooked it from, but the good side was my net was still lying on the grass back there! I stayed with the fish, walking along the towpath with it pulling me along, keeping some pressure on to try and tire her. Finally I made it back to my landing net, It didn't go for the reedbed, which was good. I increased the pressure, and the fish turned and headed straight towards me, charging along towpath margin still with a lot of power. As it came close to my feet, I just quickly pushed the net under the surface as the fish swam tight to canal margin and straight into the net. I lifted the net with the fish trying to make its escape, thrashing everywhere and soaking me in the process.

I grabbed my head torch and had a look at my prize in the net. Wow, that is wide, I thought to myself. I tried to get everything ready and weigh the fish, but he kept charging off, pulling the net with him. On the third attempt, I decided to grab a bank stick to secure the net. It was still waving its tail and charging into the front of the net while I got everything ready for the weighing. Finally I had the fish ready in the sling and zeroed the scales. The needle was bouncing from 39 to 39lb 8oz with the fish not wanting to sit still for a second. I slipped the fish into the sack and staked it out. In my excitement I forgot what the time was and rang the missus at 2am. She was not too pleased, but she did come up to give me a hand, bleary eyed. I got the scales and weigh sling reset, and this time the scales

Cluster in 1994 at 19lbs.

UK canal PB 38lb 13oz (Cluster now)

Typical canal carp.

20lbs.

23lb 15oz.

26lbs.

were shaking between 38lb 13oz and 39lb 4oz, and so I settled for 38lb 13oz. We took the photos and slipped the angry fish back into the canal's murky depths. I let my missus get back to her nice, dry, warm bed, while I just sat back on my bedchair with big, cheesy grin on my face. That was my 25th carp, including 19 over the 20lb mark from that spot. Then the area just dried up; it was as if the big fish took them all with her. I put in a lot of blanks before I realised that the group of carp had done the off and were not returning.

At first I thought it was a new fish I'd never had seen or caught before, but eventually, some days later while going through my canal photo album I managed to match the fish up with the 19lb mirror I'd caught in 1993 and named Cluster. This fish had grown 19lbs in 14 years, not bad going for a canal fish. Today I don't know if the fish still exists, I don't hear too much or see anyone else along the towpaths along the canal. I never did catch that 36lb mirror my friend caught all those years ago either. Again, is that still there, and if so, how big is it now? This keeps me going from time to time in the hope.

Sadly in more recent times, the crayfish prove to be a lot of trouble, and I have seen an otter on a couple of occasions, twice at the back of my house where I caught the 38. I can no longer prebait there, as I thought it was using it for the carp or crayfish. I don't know for sure, but I didn't want to make it easier for the otter to latch its claws onto any canal carp because of my prebaiting.

I still do the odd overnighter on the canal, just hoping to set up near them, as it's very difficult to find them now in this area, as the canal is so coloured with all the heavy boat traffic. I can still clearly remember watching a low 20lb carp grubbing about in some strands of weed at my feet on the towpath in midsummer back in the early 90s. I doubt I will ever see that again, or hearing them slurping (or clooping as they called it) on the walls of the canal or off the undersides of the pads for the snails. So now I try and guess their whereabouts, going from one location to another based on the weather conditions and time of year in the hope that the 36lb mirror from all those years ago is still about and comes along and sucks up my hookbait.

I'm sure in the future I can see myself returning to the canals on some sort of campaign, more to get away from the crowded banks than anything else though to be honest. I know there are some big and stunning looking canal carp in several of the UK canals right now, and some of them you will read about in this BC edition right here. I recently went on a recce to a canal and found a few small carp in a couple of places, so I plan a few trips to see if there is anything bigger on that canal, but for now I need to keep that under my hat. I think that is where my future canal carping lies – travelling to different canals up and down the country and probably throw in a few rivers as well along with the Belgian canals I've come to love. Next year will be my tenth anniversary fishing on the Belgium canals, and I have several trips planned already. I've written about a couple of my Belgian captures for the next edition of BC, so until then, sharp hooks.

Grand Union Canal Cracker

By Dan Sibley

With work being so busy, I have completely lost touch with my main syndicate water, having only done eight or so days up there this season. So I opted to try and keep my fishing as local as I could for the duration of the busy spell at work (easier said than done). A lot of waters around Leicester way are very busy or hard to get on, so going on some info that was given to me a good four years ago, I took a wander down the Grand Union Canal around 35 minutes drive away from work. But with them being rumours and such a long time ago, I didn't feel all that confident to say the least.

Upon arriving on the canal I stumbled across two pleasure anglers. After trying to get every bit of info about the place out of them and probably boring them to death, I moved on, still not knowing whether the old rumours I heard all those years ago were true. But the stretch definitely looked the part with nice overhanging trees, snags, boats on the far side and a marina about 500 yards down the bank.

The next day at work I spoke to a chap who lives just around the corner. His reply filled me with joy! He said, "God knows how big they are or what they are, but I take the kids down there to feed the ducks on hot days,

and they are always at the edge of the boats taking bread off the surface." One comment he did make that I really did like the sound of was: "One of them is so big that when it's sucking the bread I could throw a tennis ball in its gob."

So that night I wandered up for another look again, seeing the same two anglers, but this time I walked a lot further up towards the marina, and sure enough, I saw a good group of carp on the far side patrolling the boat line. I was buzzing, having never caught a canal carp before or even seen one. The carp were swimming in laps of the last five moored boats, so I decided to start at the edge of the very last one, partly because it was the only one that didn't look lived in. The last thing I wanted was someone banging about all night when I had baits under their boat.

About three weeks went past of religiously prebaiting 16mm Krill with hemp and whole and crushed maize to bulk it up. Finally I got down late on Friday 10/07, and flicked two rods over to the spot. I put ten or so spods over the top and sat back under the brolly buzzing for my first canal carp. The night passed without so much as a knock until at 5.30am Saturday morning the right hand rod was away. Just moments after to lifting into it, it was off! It left me feeling gutted; it was a clean cut, probably off a tin can or something like that. After that both rods had 30ft braided shock leaders on and were back out, it wasn't long before my next bite, and this time I managed to tip a lovely scaly mirror over the net – result! It was a good one too at 18lb 2oz, and I was chuffed to bits with my first carp out of the canal!

The swim became alive with fish that day fizzing and bubbling, and about 4pm that day my right hand rod pulled up and I was into a hard fighting fish, taking me up and down the stretch. Finally I managed to slip the net under it and was completely knocked back at what was lying at the bottom of my net. I knew that the rumours that I got told all those years ago were now true, as one of them was now mine. It was an immaculate common pulling the scales around to 29lb 14oz, just short of the mark, but I wasn't bothered one bit. After getting the fish back and having a few ciders, it all sunk in. I had just had a scraper 30 out of the canal! I'd had my mind set on catching scraper doubles – how wrong was I?

Unknown Possibilities

By Keith William

In 2009, after finishing university, I relocated to the famous Colne Valley. The number of gravel pits separated by rivers and a canal is quite amazing, as are the fish some of them hold. Getting a ticket for the pits proved very tricky, all having a number of restrictions, but after a few correspondences I had, in my hand, a ticket for a club lake with a known 50lb'er...

The start of my Colne Valley career was going well; I was enjoying work and catching a few carp, however, one evening I got the saddening news that the 50lb'er I was fishing for had turned up dead. I drove to the pit and gave a hand sorting bits out. The fish was inspected, as it was suspected unprepared peanuts may have been the cause – I have no idea where this rumour came from, but the other target fish had also died around the same time.

Whilst I stood at the water's edge thinking, "What now?" I met a guy call Ian. I'd seen Ian about before, but this was the first time we really spoke. We discussed where we would go from here and what tickets we could pick up. Ian told me about a place on the local canal he knew of, and so we jumped in the Vectra and headed that way – it turned out that the section of canal was less than ten minutes from my apartment and just five minutes from work! We sat by the canal and dwelled on the death of our target fish. The canal here was clear and had a slight flow as the river worked its way in and out. Along the side of the canal are some of the best carp waters in the Valley and these have been known to flood – who knows what could have ended up in the canal? Ian told me a story of an 18lb'er he had caught whilst stalking a much larger fish in the canal, which grabbed my attention.

With this and having nowhere else to fish, I thought I'd give it a go and started to bait each night after work. I was baiting with corn and hemp (now I would use boilies and tigers but as a newly qualified teacher and living away from home for the first time I couldn't afford this).

My first night on the canal I fished an area by a marina where a high bridge went over the canal. I could set up under the bridge, like a troll, and be off of the towpath. Nothing happened that first night. The baits were

slightly nipped by crays but no real issues. I did a second night, going home in the day to catch up on my marking. On this second visit, in the middle of the night, a boat decided to go into the marina. In the process it crashed into the bank, the bridge and by the time it was done it was first light and I had to pack up. Canals do have there eventful times!

I continued to bait this spot the following week. I liked being off the towpath and away from the cyclists. Friday night came, and I was back fishing. At some point in the night the alarm alerted me to a carp picking up the bait! I was straight on it. The fish scrapped hard – what had I hooked? An escapee from the pits next door? Solid. Everything locked up. I climbed over the bridge for a different angle – the fish was gone, and I brought back a flowerpot! I was gutted, but also hooked on what the canal might hold.

Next time I visited the canal I fished the spot Ian had first shown me. I hadn't prebaited this area and just flicked out a few baits. First thing in the morning I was into a fish, and soon it was in the net! My first canal carp! As I slipped the fish back another carp swam in to meet it – it was another mirror almost twice the size (possibly 35lb)! I repositioned the rods further down the canal by some snags in the direction it had swum, but of course nothing happened. It turns out the fish I had caught was the one Ian had at 18lb when he was stalking a bigger fish – this must have been the same fish I had seen. No longer was I fishing for myths and rumours – this was a big carp. It must have been from one of the lakes. I carried on with the canal catching carp to mid 20s but never saw anything bigger again.

I loved the mystery of the canal, and it's always good for a bite, however, a couple of years ago the section I fish was electro-fished and this took the mystery away from me. I'll still drop on there now and then, as the fish do move, but for me, the canal is about the unknown possibilities.

Colne Valley Escapees

By Nick Helleur

Rob's Note:

Nick has been a prolific canal carper for almost 30 years. His book 'Big Carp Hunter, Nick Helleur', which was published in 2014, is a potted version of Nick's carp fishing life and contains numerous sections on his carp fishing exploits from his early pioneering days, with his then fishing partner Dan Smith, right up to date with his many canal articles for different carp fishing magazines. It was because Nick has already covered it all here that I did not ask him to write for this book. However I have sampled a small section about his time on The Grand Union Canal just past Uxbridge where several significant fish were caught by both Dan and Nick. One was an upper thirty linear, which had escaped from Savay Lake in the 1986 floods. This fish can be seen in Steve Alcott's chapter in Tiger Bay. The second was a fish only landed by Dan and then never seen again, but it still remains a record at 42lb.

(Photograph credit) Big Carp Hunter Nick Helleur and the Internet.

We fished all round on the big, quiet pits mainly. I went back to Stockers, fished that a bit, and while I was about I fished on the canal. I could get away with it easily because it was a big pit without many carp in. Certainly from the Cons in '91 through to the mid '90s all of my fishing was on big waters and the canals and the rivers and everywhere that was free. And then bizarrely Dan had that big'un out of the canal. He went down and fished behind Farlows one night, and he phoned me in the morning and he said, "You ain't gonna believe it, but I've got a big linear in the net," and I said, "Whatcha talking about?" I can't remember if it was 28 or 31, but at the time it was monstrous, so I went down there to see it and I was amazed. I said to him, You don't reckon this could be one of the Savay fish do you; one of those that got out in the floods?" "Nah," he said, "It can't be; we're 20 miles from Savay." We were 14 locks away from Savay, but it was; it was the big linear, the one I went on to catch couple of times.

So, Roger Smith had given me that list, and we'd been looking and looking on the canal, and one day we saw a really big one. Dan asked how big I thought it was, and I said, "I don't know, but its gotta be 35 plus." It was a bright sunny day, and you could just see a silhouette of it, and it was a big carp. We got close to it, but every time we did, it would just sink into the murky canal water and we couldn't get a good look at it. Then later in the summer we were stood there having a smoke one day when we were out looking, and it popped up right in front of us. In the sunlight had a perfect view; it had big golden shoulders and we called it 'Golden Shoulders'. We never did catch it, but I had that old Savay linear at 37lb 8oz quite a few years after Dan first caught it, which was, I thought, certainly the Grand Union record at the time, but we thought it was a British canal record. There was one bigger caught in the Exeter canal that was bigger – that was 43 or something, but we never saw any pictures. We got right into that canal after I caught that big'un. That was a big carp for a canal – a big carp for anywhere at the time, but for a canal that was a giant, and out of a poxy little arm on the canal. Naturally we wanted more of those lovely old Savay carp, but it was realistically like looking for a needle in a haystack.

So we started to do a lot more looking, and then of course Dan ended up moving just round the corner there, West Drayton way, so we were there a lot. I suppose we were looking at all the bits from Savay and every stretch in between, cycling it, driving it, and watching where it just turned out from

The perfect winter spot on the canal at a warm water inlet.

A lovely canal brace. Tel and I had gone down for a look, decided to stay for the night, and I caught these. How's your luck?

The big Lin at 37, a fish with an incredible history.

Dan's Record 42lb.

the Colne. Like you'd expect with flooders, when they went, they all went in a pretty short order. It wasn't until many years later that we found that quite a lot of them had actually stayed in the river, but the brave ones, those old Galician Leney fish were just a different class. They were an older strain and I think they just had more natural purpose to keep going, and they went over the weir behind the golf course. Those fish had gone over a step weir 5ft high onto big sharp rocks, not even into deep water. That's how that linear had its stomach ripped open, and its stomach was still ripped open all those years later when I caught it. I caught it about three miles from where Dan caught it. I just saw it one day, and went back that night, and caught it – incredible carp.

Anyway further down the line, one night I was round at my girlfriend's and I got a phone call from Dan who said, "I've got Golden Shoulders." I said, "I don't believe it!" but he convinced me in the end. Anyway, I went down, and it was that big'un that we'd seen ten years before at 42lb or whatever. Funnily enough I went down the very next week and lost it, the same fish, I'm sure of it. As soon as Dan had caught it, I was back down there to have a go for it. I was having it; I knew it, and the very next morning I hooked it next to a staging where they used to fill the boats up from a diesel pump. It was like a platform that created a nice shady, snaggy area. The next day I had a bite, and it went round the platform. I held it, but it was a real strong one, and I thought, I can't let it get up any steam, but it pulled my rod flat and I couldn't do a thing to stop it; the power was incredible.

I had no option other than to hold on, but it was just too powerful and the hook hold gave, and it was gone. I knew it was that one; it was just too powerful to be anything else. It wasn't the linear; he wasn't around there. It was that big'un with a group of five or six smaller fish. I'd lost it, and that was my last chance at it because it ultimately disappeared, but I never knew for sure where it went. Rumours are that it got stolen, but we will never know the truth for sure.

When that fish disappeared, I lost a lot of my motivation, and because of what happened at the canal I began to be more careful about the fish I chose to target.

Basingstoke Canal Record

By Danny Champion

The Basingstoke canal is probably one of the most underestimated carp venues in the southwest. I have always thought about the history of the canal as I've walked down the twists and turns. Like most anglers we try to find out as much as we can about the history of the venue. So here are the facts: The Basingstoke canal was conceived as an agricultural waterway to connect northeast Hampshire with London. Construction took place in 1787 and took seven years to complete, finally finishing in 1794. The waterway played a vital role in the First World War in 1914. The Royal Engineers took over the waterway, and it was used as an inland transport system carrying military hardware to Aldershot. As traffic slowed after WW1 the canal was sold privately in 1923. In 1949 the canal was sold to the new Basingstoke canal company. They tried to manage the canal by selling fishing tickets, encouraging houseboat moorings and encouraging unpowered pleasure craft. But with the backlog of maintenance in 1964 the canal was almost totally derelict. The canal would be left in this way for the next ten years. In 1974 Surrey County and Hampshire Council took the canal over and started the restoration work, working in partnership with the canal society. On May 10th 1991 the canal was reopened by his royal highness the Duke of Kent. It took millions of voluntary hours with funding coming from the county councils.

Trying to catch one of the elusive canal carp can be extremely difficult I have spent days walking my fishing mate Avid (the Jack Russell) without seeing a single fish. If you are serious about trying to catch a canal carp you need to be dedicated and put all your time into it, but it can be done. I am expecting my second child so time for me can be limited, but at the same time you have to think to yourself how much you want it. Luckily for me I have a very understanding partner/permission officer. If I were approaching a new canal the two things I would pay the most attention to would be time spent and the main features.

As a whole, locating carp on a canal is extremely difficult with miles of muddy brown waterways for the fish to move up and down, not to mention the nightmare of it being a public footpath with dogs jumping

10lb canal common.

20lb canal common.

into your swim, the late night stragglers walking home from the pub and cyclists speeding around every bend! I've found getting up at first light to be a huge advantage. You would be amazed at how much of a difference a few hours in the morning can make. The amount of fish activity is staggering. Overhanging trees and boat turning points are always a good start. There are several flashes along the way that always hold a large amount of fish. I try to avoid barges and narrow boats, as they are a haven for smaller fish. On the Basingstoke canal the bigger fish move in twos, and are clearly not moving with the smaller shoals of carp.

Capture of the 40lb 2oz canal mirror.

It was a hot summer's day when I finished work late in the afternoon. I couldn't decide if I had the energy to get down to the canal. But like the keen angler I am, I decided to go home, get my gear and get down on the spot I had be prebaiting for the last three weeks. When I arrived I couldn't hold back my excitement as I could see two large specimens cruising in and out of the overhanging trees I had been prebaiting. One of the fish I recognised as the large 30lb-plus common I would later go on to catch, but I had never seen the other fish, which looked like a whale! I set my rods up about 20 yards down from the spot trying my best to be as quiet as I could, but by the time I had set up a few runners and cyclists had been through, and the fish were gone. I was devastated.

I spent the rest of the evening setting my kit up, thinking to myself, what if? That evening after seeing the two big specimens, I decided to bait heavily in an effort to bring them back to my swim. I chopped up over 5kg of mixed Cell and Hybrid, putting it down the 20yd stretch I was fishing. The night was uneventful, but I tied new rigs for the morning. My rig of choice was a D-rig tied with a large size 2 Krank. Knowing the fish must have seen a lot of corn from other anglers, I decided to use an Evolution corn stack, as this critically balanced the rig without any need for putty to weigh the hook down. At 4am I woke up to place my rigs on the spot that was now fizzing. I took my 12m baiting pole out, placed my rig with a few freebies in and pushed the spoon out as slowly as I could. Just as I hit my spot a fish rolled inches away from the spoon, I didn't want to tip the spoon in case I spooked any of the carp, so I decided to throw a few boilies

over the spot to push out any of the fish. About ten minutes later I tipped the spoon over and felt the rig hit the gravel spot.

I sat there watching a kingfisher whizzing up and down the stretch of canal. I had to sit on my hands, as I could see bubbles coming up right over my rig. I didn't have to wait long before the left hand rod ripped off producing a scale perfect 22lb 5oz common. I was over the moon! It wasn't one of the bigger fish I had seen, but it was still a beautiful fish nonetheless. The weather was a lot cooler than the previous day, so I was looking forward to the day I had ahead of me. I placed my rigs back out and started to prep more rigs for the rest of the day. Hours went past without any sign of the carp, but I decided to stick it out, as I new they felt comfortable on the spot. I didn't think what happened next was possible!

The sound of a one-toner from the Delkim and the water erupting made me jump out of my chair, hitting into what I can only be described as striking into a brick wall. In all my years fishing I had never felt a fish so powerful! It was like a dolphin trying to leap out of the water, as it had nowhere to go. I found myself trying to keep the fish from pulling me into the snags. I somehow managed to gain a few metres on the fish, but boy was it a mistake! The fish shot left 30yds down the canal. The clutch on the reel was making a noise I'd never heard before. I knew there were several snags to the left, so I had no other choice but to go in after it fully clothed. I kept as close as I could to the margin, following the fish down, still putting a huge bend in my rod. I playing the fish for about another 20 minutes, trying to gain line, but every time I thought I was getting somewhere it reminded me who was in charge and ripped across the surface of the water.

I remember I had people stopping behind me asking what it was that I had hooked, but I couldn't answer them, as I was trying my hardest to land the beast. Eventually I managed to wear the fish out and get it within netting distance, but the only problem was my net was about ten yards back down the canal! I slowly moved backwards towards the net. At this time the fish was still in control, and if it wanted to go all it had to do was flick its tail and I'd be helpless. 30 minutes into the fight I had the net in the water ready. For years to come I will always remember the relief when

22lb canal common.

REEZER
ANGE
THE ANGLER'S CHOICE
Betalin
KORDA
KRANK
4
KORDA
IQ2
EXTRA SOFT FLUOROCARBON
IMPROVED STRENGTH &
ABRASION RESISTANCE
20lb 0.47 20m
mainline

35lb 6oz Basingstoke canal common.

I slipped the net under the fish. I was looking down at what can only be called an angler's dream – not just a 40, but a historical old canal carp.

I phoned a friend with excitement, and within ten minutes he was on the footpath helping me do the weighing and photos. When I saw the weight my jaw dropped, and my brain didn't register what I had just accomplished. Kneeling on the towpath holdling the specimen, we both looked in awe at the size of the paddle and the pecs that were close to a foot long! The colours were outstanding: greys, reds and browns. The release was just as memorable as the fight. I felt privileged to catch and see such an amazing creature. I packed up and went home with the biggest smile on my face, knowing I'd never beat that!

It was exactly a week later that I decided to get up at first light to see if I could get the other large common I saw. I placed my rigs on the same spot I had the 40 from and set my bivvy up for a couple of hours' sleep. I had my back turned for two seconds and a narrow boat took both of my rods

Basingstoke canal record.

out. The owner of the boat just looked forward and didn't have the balls to turn around a say sorry. I was fuming! All he had to do was slow down so I could lower my rods to let him pass! That's just one of the problems you have to deal with on the canal, most of which can be avoid by just being polite and courteous. I had to replace all the end tackle on both rods, as I was totally wiped out.

Thirty minutes later I had my rods good to go, and I proceeded to drop both rigs off using the baiting pole. I sat there thinking to myself that anything there was properly gone after all the commotion. Two hours passed with no indication of fish. I knew my bait was still there, as coots kept diving down and picking it up. All I can remember is seeing one bubble come to the surface and then the water imploding as I was in to another large specimen. The fight was once again all in the carp's favour. I had no room to play the fish and could only try and keep as much line out the water as I could. This fish felt different to the others I had caught on the canal; it stayed deep and plodded along. It never picked up any speed; it just refused to come up from the depths. I thought to myself how nice it would be if every fish fought like this. This is what I go fishing for – so many day ticket waters have carp that give up the minute they are hooked, but these canal carp fought like it was for their lives!

I slipped the net under what I could only described as a solid dark gold common. When I weighed the fish I was chuffed. It was an impressive 35lb 6oz common – another PB from the canal and another piece of history. The fish was scale perfect with a slight graze on its left flank probably from the recent spawning. I released the fish after taking the photos with thoughts of the age of the specimen and if it had ever been caught before. I had never seen this fish in photos. I decided to carry on fishing till dusk and had a 27lb mirror – another lump from the canal. I've been asked several times if I think there's a 50 in there. Anything's possible, as I've just proved.

Canals are difficult waters to fish when targeting carp. Here are a few ways to make your fishing more effective: Buy a baiting spoon; they are a way of getting to the places you could never cast and a way to keep disturbance down. These come in all different sizes, but I would advise buying a Colnemere Developments 12m baiting pole – its strong and reliably built for the job. Other models I have seen make hard work trying to attach each section, as you are pushing your rig out and they tend to bend and eventually break.

Don't be afraid to put in large amounts of bait on areas where you have seen carp. A 30lb carp will think nothing of eating half a kilo of boilies in one sitting. The amount of other pest fish needs to be accounted for as well – bream, roach, rudd, tench and not to mention crayfish. Spread the bait over a large area to try channel the feeding fish into your baited area.

Any good quality boilie will work on the canal, but try stay away from fishmeals, as this is more likely to attract the crays. Don't forget sweetcorn, as the fish feed on this the most. Match the hatch with your hookbait as well – the Evolution corn stacks dipped in Hinders Betalin not only stops the crays pinching your hookbait, but they have a natural feel/look to them. Rig choice is a minefield these days. All I can suggest is fish with what you feel comfortable with, but beef it up. Remember canals are full of snags, so instead of using a size 6-8, go big or go home. I have had a 50% catch increase using size 2 hooks. I know for some this may seem overkill, but it works, and that's all I expect of a rig. Give your local canal a go; you never know what could be lurking in the depths!

Chapter 11

Overseas Canal Carping

photo of the big common he showed me looked stunning. I thanked him for showing me the photos and the information, and he headed off home, as he had been down for a midweek session.

Later I was to find out he thought I was mad coming over to only do one or two nights on this particular stretch, and he was probably right in all honesty. Eventually it was time to cook myself some food and then call it a night, as a hint of frost was on the leaf covered ground, and it was time to get myself wrapped up in my sleeping bag. Also it did get really dark in that pine forest.

Around 9pm, my right hand alarm startled me, and I fumbled around in the dark to find my hiking boots. With them half on I hopped over to the rods and struck while the indicator was jammed into the bite alarm and instantly felt the power of the fish on the end as he went on a blistering run. After an age with the fish making several runs, me feeling the power of it, and the mainline taking a battering on the stony margin riddled with mussels, he was starting to tire. After a moment's panic with my net getting tangled in some marginal brambles, I got it free and managed to net my first Belgian canal carp. I then finally slipped my boots on properly and grabbed my headtorch to see my prize. This long, big-framed fish filled the full width and bottom of my net.

I got myself together and hoisted the fish onto the waiting mat, then unhooked and weighed it. The needle went just past the 56lb mark on my 56lb Nash scales! I settled on 56lbs 4oz, as the needle looked to be about that much over, maybe a tiny bit more. I ran down to the guy set up by sluice 5, and he duly came up and gave me a hand with the photos. They were not the best, but we did the best we could in the darkness. I think I needed to hit the gym, as I'd not held a fish of that weight before and struggled to be honest. It was too early in the night for me to sack for that long, and so I was glad to slip him back, shake hands with the Dutch guy for assisting me, and then put the kettle on for celebratory cuppa, and tell all my mates what I'd just caught – truly unbelievable to me. Sadly this fish died in 2013.

Tale of the Second Fifty

The following year I had already done a trip during the spring, and had been very lucky in catching four fish to 39lbs, one of them being a 34lb common coming from the 4-5 stretch on the KK. I had bumped into Jo again, and he couldn't believe what I was showing him on my camera – two nights and two fish on this hard stretch of canal where anglers have gone for years without a bite. The first two nights of the trip, I fished a different canal, the VK, but without any success. I had baited up the 4-5KK on each afternoon, planning to move the short distance on the third day of the weeklong trip. I placed my left hand rod on the far margin where I'd caught the 56 this time last year, and the right hand rod on the nearside margin to my right where I'd caught the 34 back in the spring. It gave me a lot of confidence knowing I was fishing both rods now on productive spots. I also placed a small handful of baits at several intervals along the canal's margins. My thinking was to get the fish confident on the baits before reaching my hookbait and making a mistake. The weather was milder and a lot wetter this autumn but a lot more carpy.

Just after midnight I had an aborted take on the close-in margin rod. I wound in and everything appeared fine, with the hook still sharp. Nothing else happened during the night, and once the first barge came through I dropped the other rod in the near margin for the day as well. I was sitting there just trying to picture the big common that Jo had shown me on the previous trip. Jo was due to pop down in a couple nights' time, and I was thinking of sending him a text, asking him to see if he could drop a picture of the common off, or send me a copy over the phone to keep me motivated for this trip and for future trips. Just before the light started to fade again for my second night, I baited up around six spots with just a few boilies for couple of a hundred yards to my left on the near margin. I then got my left hand rod back out on the opposite margin and topped up the spot with around six baits just to its left. I left the right hand rod alone, but topped up with some boilies, tigers and hemp.

Just before midnight the left hand rod was away with a slow but steady take. I struck into the fish sideways as I was using back leads, and felt the fish instantly and the rod took on its battle curve. It felt a very powerful fish, but did not fight like the previous two fish from this stretch. The fish took a few runs and used its weight to hold bottom, but I got it in to the

58lb.

56lb 4oz.

margins fairly quickly. Then the fish came alive and got caught round my other line somehow, even though I was using back leads. I flicked the bail arm open on the offending rod and kept the pressure on the fish. Slowly I made progress on the fish, and it looked like a common boiling under the crystal clear water, but it was so dark I wasn't 100% sure.

Eventually with some difficulty I got the fish into the net. I had problems lifting the net, as it had got caught on a bramble bush again, and it was being held down by the other line it had got tangled up with. I put my knee on the landing net handle and stretched for my head torch by the bivvy. I bent over the side of the canal and flicked on the head torch, and then it hit me! Staring up at me was the big common, and it just swallowed up the bottom of the net. Judging by the length and width from above, this surely was going to be my biggest fish ever. I sorted out the mess with the lines, broke down the net, rolled it up, and somehow managed to get the fish and net on the unhooking mat floating in the margins. Then I lifted the fish out of the water with a bit of a struggle. With my new scales, the needle settled on 58lbs exactly. I then placed the fish in the sack and sent a text to pretty much everyone.

Eggy, a friend I made during my last trip, was on the VK canal around the corner and said he would cycle round in the morning to help with the pictures. I obviously didn't sleep for a single second, buzzing and getting up every few minutes to make sure the fish was ok. A gallon of coffee later, Eggy came round in the morning during a break in the rain, and we took some pictures. The fish was just perfect for me, never playing up. I then returned her to the canal and packed up for the final time on that particular stretch. I wouldn't need those pictures from Jo anymore, as I now had my own! What a fish.

Tale of the Third Fifty

It's taken me some time and several trips to manage another 50lb-plus fish from Belgium. I had several good and stunning looking fish to mid forty over the last nine years fishing the Belgian canals, but it was not until this year I finally bagged another lump and from a different canal this time. I had already made my plans before I'd even set off. I usually have two trips to Belgium each year, one in the spring and one in the autumn, but this year

I was only going the once in the spring. I had eight nights at my disposal, and it didn't actually start to plan...

I'd arrived at my first canal to bait up a couple of spots for the end of my trip, then headed to my intended canal, the VK, home to some monstrous sized carp up to 80lb. VK had no sluices and was connected to the KK and the massive Albert Canal, which is about the width of the Thames in London. It has depths in excess of 20ft for the big working barges that use it daily, carrying sand, gravel, fuel and shipping containers. VK also had a very large sand pit in excess of 100 acres connected directly to the canal that was private fishing where the barges carrying sand were loaded up with sand and then headed off in either direction along the canal. The carp like this area, but it is very deep lake, and is generally colder than the canal, so it's not an area they use so much in the spring/summer months or for spawning, when they are on the main canal.

I arrived at the canal just before midnight on a Friday. It was May bank holiday weekend, but in Belgium they had the holiday on Friday not Monday, and after passing more than thirty bivvies, it was time to revert to plan B. I returned to the canal near Antwerp where I had baited up an hour or so before. I did two nights – a night on each prebaited spot, but nothing occurred. On the Monday morning, I baited up with 5kg of bait and then left for the VK. It was now empty, but for a couple of anglers by the VK/KK crossing. I chose to fish an area where I'd had some success the two previous springs about a mile down from the lake opening. There was no one in the area, so I dropped everything off, and then dropped my car to the nearest road bridge, as you will get fined for driving on the paths along the canals now. I got set up and flicked both rods out with just stringers for the day, as there had been a lot of anglers on at the weekend, which meant a lot of bait as well. That evening a couple of anglers turned up to my left and right, which was not ideal, but I'd caught in this situation in the past.

The following morning, I'd not seen anything of note. It didn't appear that any of the other anglers had either, and three of the four soon left for work. The wind had changed and had picked up, blowing down towards the VK/KK crossing, so I chose to pack up again and move further up to

53lb 15oz.

53lb 15oz other side.

somewhere else where I'd had some success in the past during the spring period. While I was packing, I was sure I saw a common show 100 or so yards downwind of me, just backing up my choice to move.

I turned up at a sort of bottleneck at the top of the canal, where it turns into the Dessel canal before its first lock. This stretch is a lot narrower than the VK – VK being around 60 yards across, whereas the Dessel is probably only 20 yards or so across. This does mean the barges are very close to you. I didn't actually put any rods to begin with; I just set up, got a few rigs tied up and went for a walk to see if I could find any fish. The only fish I found was a group of bream spawning in a fenced off area of a mooring bay just up to my left on the other side of a road bridge. This is fenced off specifically for spawning fish, and it has a couple of narrow channels for fish to enter/exit.

I've never caught during the day in this area before, only at night when the barges stop, but for some reason, I decided to place a single rod down to my right facing the entrance to the VK/KK crossing with half a dozen chopped boilies. Then I sat back in my bivvy having lunch and then doing some reading. A few barges had chugged by in both directions, and I had a few bleeps on the rod, so I went to inspect it. I found a load of weed and debris around the line entering the water, so I flicked the alarm off, cleaned off the debris and placed the rod back on the alarm... Note: forgetting to switch the alarm back on!

I then noticed to my left in the middle of the canal something floating on the surface. It was a small, dead common of about 3-5lbs, probably brought down with the barges. Then I noticed a larger object floating not far from my right hand rod and went to inspect, fearing the worst. It turned out to be someone's pet cat dead and bloated up, so it looked like a dead carp to me to begin with.

I walked back to my bivvy and rods, and as I approached the line looked very odd. The hanger was on the floor limp, and the line was now pointing to the left by the bridge, not to my right – damn! Strike! Luckily I felt the power of the fish, as it had already made 30 or so yards on me, and was close the bridge. I chose to walk off in its direction, keeping the tension, and before long I was standing on the opposite side of the bridge 50 or so yards away playing a fish in the mooring bay. I had no choice but to follow it, with brick walled margins, scattered with snags, and a large metal mooring for boats to the immediate left of the bridge.

The fish tried to make sanctuary under a couple of small barges moored on the opposite side, which were working on the canal's bankside at the time, and then it headed off towards the spawning channel. I had to put the brakes on again, and clamped hold of my spool to stop its run. It turned and boiled very close, and then turned and made its way back towards the barges, where I had to clamp down once again. Eventually it was back in the middle channel, turning left and right, slowly making some progress, and then it kited to my right and back under the bridge towards my setup thankfully, as my landing net was still there.

I kept the pressure on, and tried to keep the fish from the bottom, as I'd lost a fish in the past from under the bridge, possibly due to a sunken bicycle. Finally I was standing next to my landing net and could play the fish out, and after a few runs and boils on the surface, I got to see that I was attached to a right old lump of a mirror carp. I was getting tired now, with my arms aching, so it was a big relief when I netted the fish, and what

a fish! It was stunning! The scales were so random. I secured the net, and then with shaking hands grabbed my phone and sent texts out to some of my Belgian friends, as assistance would be required. I got the mat and sling sorted, weighed the fish at an ounce short of 54lbs, and then placed the fish in the recovery sling.

My friend, who I'd met on my first ever trip back in 2007, drove the hour to get to me and did the honours with the photos and video. We were both like, wow, look at the scaling and the length of this fish! It was actually longer than my recovery sling, but I didn't have a tape measure on me to record its length. The fish was returned, and I asked several locals if they knew the fish, but none had seen it before, so it was a potentially unknown 50 – just amazing! Still today, as I write this, it's got to be up there for me as one of the most stunning carp I've been privileged to see in my arms. After that I moved onto another canal, and Jo popped by again with a couple of celebratory Jupilers (Belgian beer). I had a couple of small ones and lost a right old lump, with my knees shaking during the fight before the line parted, and so I will have to return to make amends!

Next year will make ten years consecutively fishing the Belgium canals for me, hoping to catch my fiftieth Belgium carp. It was the big fish from KK7-8 that got me inspired to go out there originally, and I've still not caught from 7-8, although I have only fished it a couple of times. I will be making plans for next year to visit the stretch again and hopefully be lucky. Sharp hooks, everyone!